LAW AND THE STUDENT PRESS

LAW

AND THE

STUDENT PRESS

George E. Stevens John B. Webster

THE IOWA STATE UNIVERSITY PRESS / AMES

1973

GEORGE E. STEVENS is assistant professor of communication and chairman of the journalism program at Purdue University. He received the B.A. degree from Pacific University and the M.A. and Ph.D. degrees from the University of Minnesota. He was a reporter and editor on Oregon and Washington newspapers and for five years was adviser to student publications at the University of Cincinnati. At Purdue he teaches courses in news law and high school publications advising, and he is a member of the board of directors of the Purdue *Exponent*. He has published in a dozen journals in the areas of news law and journalism history.

JOHN B. WEBSTER is assistant professor of communication at Purdue University. He received the B.A. degree from Arkansas State University, the M.J. degree from the University of Texas, and the Ph.D. degree from the University of Minnesota. His journalism background includes printing, reporting, and editorial work for community newspapers in Missouri and Arkansas. He is a former publications editor for the Arkansas Industrial Research Center in Little Rock and for the Federal Reserve Bank in Minneapolis. At Purdue he teaches courses in high school publications advising, public affairs reporting, and press and society.

© 1973 The Iowa State University Press
Ames, Iowa 50010. All rights reserved
Composed and printed by The Iowa State University Press
First edition, 1973

Stevens, George E   1936–
  Law and the student press.
  Bibliography: p.
  1. College and school journalism—Law and legislation—United States.
I. Webster, John B., 1927–   joint author.   II. Title.
KF4165.S7   343′.73′0998   73–12276
ISBN 0-8138-0875-8

FOR L.J., J.H., AND P.J.

CONTENTS

PREFACE   ix

CHAPTER ONE: CENSORSHIP   3

CHAPTER TWO: LIBEL   26

CHAPTER THREE: OBSCENITY   46

CHAPTER FOUR: CONTEMPT   57

CHAPTER FIVE: ADVERTISING   63

CHAPTER SIX: COPYRIGHT   71

CHAPTER SEVEN: ACCESS TO INFORMATION   76

CHAPTER EIGHT: SEPARATE PUBLISHING GROUPS   84

CHAPTER NINE: OFF-CAMPUS DISTRIBUTION   95

CHAPTER TEN: SELECTED PROBLEMS   101
        Privacy, 101
        Taxation, 102
        Broadcasting, 104
        Postal Regulations, 105

APPENDICES   109
        A: *Joint Statement on the Rights and Freedoms
           of Students—Student Publications,* 109
        B: *American Civil Liberties Union Statement on
           Freedom of the High School Press,* 110

APPENDIX C: *American Bar Association Statement on Freedom of the Campus Press,* 111

D: *High School Newspaper Policy Statement,* 112

E: *College Communications Board Constitution and Bylaws,* 114

F: *Articles of Incorporation for a College Separate Publishing Group,* 123

G: *Campus Broadcast Station Policy Statement,* 128

H: *Excerpts from Federal Communications Commission Rules and Regulations for Educational Broadcast Stations,* 133

I: *Distribution Guidelines for High School Publications,* 136

J: *Excerpts from Post Office Second-Class Mailing Permit Regulations,* 137

NOTES 143

NOTES ON SOURCES 153

INDEX OF CASES 155

INDEX OF NAMES 157

PREFACE

WHEN UPHEAVALS OVER STUDENT RIGHTS struck many high schools and colleges during the latter part of the 1960s and the early years of the 1970s, one of the major issues was a demand for free expression in student publications. For the first time, courts ruled on cases involving the rights of student journalists.

Law and the Student Press deals primarily with these volatile years. We have brought together cases and legal decisions involving the student press (high school, college, underground) to show how the law has been applied to school officials and student journalists. In some situations, we have drawn upon non-school decisions to provide guidance. We have also included suggestions for those connected with student publications in the hope that they may not only stay out of court but may work together harmoniously during a time of change and uncertainty in colleges and high schools.

We did not attempt to write a book on general press law. Those who need a more detailed general background than that we provide should consult one of the books listed in our "Notes on Sources." Throughout our book we have attempted to answer a question often asked by advisers, administrators, and student publication staff members: "How does press law affect me?"

We would like to thank J. Robert Walker and James Kopka for their help in the preparation of this book.

G. E. S.
J. B. W.

LAW AND THE STUDENT PRESS

CHAPTER ONE

CENSORSHIP

CENSORSHIP OF STUDENT PUBLICATIONS is one of the most emotional issues in the controversy over student rights in high schools and colleges.

Arguments favoring tight controls over the campus press usually center around (1) the responsibilities of high schools and colleges as legal publishers of school-sponsored periodicals and (2) the fact that student journalists are immature and need guidance. There is no doubt that a high school or college is legally responsible for the contents of its publications. "The only exception is where the publication can be proved without question to be completely independent of [school] financing and control," emphasizes Vernon W. Smith.[1] And the Maryland State Board of Education points out:

> [T]raditionally public schools have been considered "in loco parentis" to [those] who attend school. When children are minors, they must have parental consent and guidance in much of their activity. . . . In the absence of the parent in the school environment, the school must be allowed to exercise mature judgment such as would be exercised by a mature parent.[2]

Some faculty members maintain that constitutional freedom of the press guarantees do not apply to a staff member, reporter, or editor of any publication—student or professional. The guarantees, they argue, are

> only to the publisher, to the one who is willing to pay, to risk his investment, to see his right of free expression translated into the print medium. . . . In simple truth, then,

censorship becomes a fact only when restrictions are imposed from outside the paper's ownership . . . censorship
is the wrong word to use with regard to limitations on expression imposed by adviser, faculty member, or administrator.[3]

Those who favor few controls over expression in the student
press usually point to the educational advantages of uninhibited
communication. "Censorship of news and editorial opinion is a
reprehensible doctrine since it destroys a fundamental tool of the
democratic educational process: freedom of discussion and debate," said Buell G. Gallaher, president of City College of New
York.[4] William Birenbaum, president of Staten Island Community College, told his faculty and students: "Experimentation is
implicit in learning. Making misjudgments and committing in-
discretions are to be expected as part of learning. Censorship
does not promote the conditions necessary for education; rather
it subverts those conditions."[5]

Robert J. Glessing believes that college and high school publications "should be tools of amateur journalists who are stretch-
ing to become professionals. A student must learn that freedom
of the press is not just idle rhetoric but is truly administrative
policy and reality."[6] Mark J. Green declares: "By teaching the
young our constitutional guarantees and then by denying these
rights to them, students will acquire the degree of cynicism and
contempt for adult hypocrisy now so rampant in our country."[7]

The American Association of University Professors (AAUP),
the American Civil Liberties Union (ACLU), and the American
Bar Association (ABA) have issued statements condemning censorship of student publications (see Appendices A, B, and C). But
all three groups believe that steps must be taken to protect schools
from libel suits or abuses of unrestrained expression. The AAUP
counsels college editors to avoid "libel, indecency, undocumented
allegations, attacks on personal integrity, and the techniques of
harassment and innuendo."[8] The ACLU believes that neither
adviser nor principal should prohibit the publication or distribution of material in high schools except when the health and safety
of students or the educational process is threatened, or when the
material might be of a libelous nature.[9] The ABA endorses
limited review of campus publications "solely as a reasonable precaution against the publication of matter which would expose
the institution to liability."[10]

As censorship of student publications became a much-debated issue in the mid-1960s, advisers and administrators did not stop censoring school-sponsored publications, especially in high schools and small colleges. Censorship did not seem as prevalent at large colleges and universities where freedom of expression is a well-established tradition. In a mid-1960s study of newspapers at 60 large colleges, only seven editors reported significant administrative controls.[11] However, in a 1965 survey of 91 principals and 92 publication advisers in Los Angeles County public and parochial high schools, 41 percent of the principals and 60 percent of the advisers admitted they had exercised their powers of censorship at least once. All the advisers and 73 of the 91 principals read copy prior to publication.[12] A study released in 1969 of 177 student newspapers at small (2,500 enrollment or under) colleges revealed that 78 percent of the newspapers had been subjected to at least attempted censorship during the previous two years. Twenty-eight percent reported that a person other than a student staff member (usually an adviser or president of the college) had censored an item during the two-year period.[13]

Unhappy with the limitations on expression in their high schools and colleges, some student journalists started turning to the courts in the latter part of the 1960s. The judicial rulings in these cases are far from definitive, but they do provide some guidance for administrators, advisers, and students. In general, the decisions have favored students and overruled unreasonable school policies which interfere with their free expression rights.

JUDICIAL DECISIONS

TINKER

In 1969 the U.S. Supreme Court, for the first time in its history, decided a case that dealt with student rights of free expression not connected with religious matters. The case, *Tinker* v. *Des Moines Independent Community School District*,[14] did not directly involve a student publication; but the Court's reasoning in *Tinker* has been the basis for subsequent decisions by lower courts on the rights of student journalists in high schools and colleges.

The case arose when the Tinker youngsters, ages 15 and 13, wore black armbands to Des Moines (Iowa) public schools as a protest against the Vietnam war. School officials asked the Tinkers to remove the armbands and suspended them when they refused. The Tinkers then brought suit, maintaining that their constitutional rights of free expression had been abridged. Two lower courts upheld the schools' action on the grounds that it was a reasonable way to enforce school discipline, and the Tinkers appealed to the Supreme Court.

The high court ruled in favor of the Tinkers. Their wearing of armbands, the Court noted, involved First Amendment rights akin to "pure speech." Justice Fortas, writing the majority opinion, ruled that school officials have the authority to prescribe and control conduct of students, but that

> [i]n our system, state-operated schools may not be enclaves of totalitarianism. School officials do not possess absolute authority over their students. Students in school as well as out of school are "persons" under our Constitution. They are possessed of fundamental rights which the state must respect. . . . In the absence of a specific showing of constitutionally valid reasons to regulate their speech, students are entitled to freedom of expression of their views.

Intercommunication among students is "an important part of the educational process," Justice Fortas wrote. He emphasized that

> [i]n order for the State in the person of school officials to justify prohibition of a particular expression of opinion, it must be able to show that its action was caused by something more than a mere desire to avoid the discomfort and unpleasantness that always accompany an unpopular viewpoint. Certainly where there is no finding and no showing that engaging in the forbidden conduct would materially and substantially interfere with the requirements of appropriate discipline in the operation of the school, the prohibition cannot be sustained.

SULLIVAN

Lower courts soon applied the Supreme Court's reasoning to cases involving high school underground newspapers.

In a 1969 case, *Sullivan* v. *Houston Independent School District*,[15] a U.S. District Court overruled school authorities in Texas who had suspended two high school underground journalists for distributing a newspaper critical of the Houston school system. The newspaper, *Pflashlyte*, reported a sarcastic speech by a hypothetical school administrator who said, in part: "For mah fine capacity to suppress ideas, ah have been awarded this school and yore minds." A principal had ordered the students to stop circulating *Pflashlyte;* when they refused he established rules forbidding the paper's distribution, then suspended Sullivan and another student from Sharpstown High School in Houston.

School officials claimed that students were reading the newspaper during class time and also argued that there was an organized student attempt to overthrow the city's school system. Distribution of the newspaper had to be stopped, the defendants maintained, to prevent further "infiltration."

The court, however, agreed with the plaintiffs' contention that the action of school officials had denied them their free expression rights. Students have the right to produce and distribute newspapers on and off campus as long as they do not substantially disrupt school operations, said the court, and the disturbances caused by *Pflashlyte* were "minor and relatively few in number." The court noted that only one student "discipline card" that was in any way related to the newspaper was filled out at the high school.

The suspension of students using rules drawn up after they started distributing their newspaper was a denial of due process, the court said, and the district was ordered to reinstate the two suspended students and enjoined from carrying out similar suspensions in the future. However, the court did indicate that if "precise and narrowly drawn regulations" were established, publication and distribution of student periodicals could be barred if these activities "materially and substantially disrupt the normal operations of the school."

SCOVILLE

In 1970 a U.S. Circuit Court of Appeals relied on *Tinker* when it ruled that high school officials in Joliet, Illinois, could not penalize underground newspaper editors unless their activities led school authorities to "reasonably . . . forecast substantial disruption of or material interference with school activities."

The case, *Scoville* v. *Board of Education,*[16] grew out of the publication and distribution in 1968 of about 60 copies of the underground newspaper *Grass High* in Joliet's Central High School. *Grass High* suggested that students not accept school "propaganda," called school regulations "asinine," accused a dean of having a "sick mind," and also commented that "oral sex may prevent tooth decay."

The Board of Education expelled two of *Grass High*'s editors under a regulation that allowed expulsion of pupils "guilty of gross disobedience or misconduct." The students brought suit, alleging violation of their constitutional rights of free speech.

Prior to *Tinker* a U.S. District Court upheld the board's action. The district court said that the editors' actions "amounted to an immediate advocacy of, and incitement to, disregard of school administrative procedures," and that distribution of *Grass High* was a substantial threat to effective operation of Central High. Furthermore, the court noted that

> [p]articularly in elementary and secondary schools, the state has a compelling interest in maintaining an atmosphere conducive to an orderly program of classroom learning, and to respect for legitimate and necessary administrative rules.

After the *Tinker* decision, a three-judge panel of a U.S. Court of Appeals still affirmed the district court decision. The panel noted that the objectives of an editorial in *Grass High* "were incitement of students to ignore accepted school procedures and the condemnation of the school." The panel was satisfied that the content of *Grass High* might lead school officials to forecast "disruption of or material interference with school activities."

The entire U.S. Court of Appeals for the Seventh Circuit then ruled on the case and reversed the previous decisions. The court of appeals said that the district court had no factual basis on which it could make a forecast of disruption or interference. For example, no evidence was presented on the impact *Grass High* actually had in the school. Even though *Grass High* showed "a disrespect and tasteless attitude toward authority," the sale of 60 copies of the paper did not by itself justify suppressing it. "That plaintiffs may have intended their criticism to substantially disrupt or materially interfere with the enforcement of school policies is of no significance per se under the *Tinker* test," the opinion said. When school rules infringe on freedom of expression, the court pointed out that school officials have the burden of justifying them.

EISNER

In another important case, *Eisner* v. *Stamford Board of Education*,[17] the issue was whether a student newspaper could be distributed in a public high school without first being submitted to the school administration for approval of its contents.

The plaintiffs, students at Rippowan High School in Stamford, Connecticut, published an "independent mimeographed newspaper" called the *Stamford Free Press*. When they attempted to circulate the paper on school grounds, they ran into a Board of Education policy that prohibited distribution of printed or written material unless the school administration approved. The students contended that such advance approval was constitutionally prohibited "prior restraint" on expression.

U. S. District Court Judge Robert C. Zampano agreed. He found the Stamford board's policy "unconstitutional" and "unenforceable" and wrote:

> The Board of Education has the duty under Connecticut law, and the right under *Tinker,* to punish conduct by the student, in class or out of it, which for any reason—whether it stems from time, place, or type of behavior—materially disrupts classwork or involves substantial disorder or invasion of the rights of others. But this right and duty does not include blanket prior restraint; the risk taken if a few abuse their First Amendment rights of free speech and press is outweighed by the far greater risk run by suppressing free speech and press among the young.

Zampano noted that school administrators must have "wide latitude in formulating rules and guidelines to govern student conduct," and that "students must conform to reasonable regulations" which intrude on freedom of expression. But in the *Eisner* case

> the [board's] regulations provide none of the procedural safeguards designed to obviate the dangers of a censorship system. Among other things, the regulations do not specify the manner of submission, the exact party to whom the material must be submitted, the time within which a decision must be rendered; nor do they provide for an adversary proceeding of any type or for a right of appeal.

Zampano added that student newspapers were "valuable educational tools" and "peaceful channels of student protest which should be encouraged, not suppressed."

The U.S. Court of Appeals for the Second Circuit upheld the district court's ruling that the existing Stamford policy could not be enforced, but it also upheld the authority of school officials to require students to obtain prior approval to distribute publications if the school's rules contain safeguards for student rights. The appeals court noted that certain language—for example libelous, obscene, or fighting words (those that invite confrontation)—could be subject to prior restraint; and "it would be highly disruptive to the educational process if a secondary school principal were required to take a school newspaper editor to court every time the principal reasonably anticipated disruption and sought to restrain its cause."

However, the court ruled that schools should require prior submission "only when there is to be a *substantial* distribution of written material, so that it can reasonably be anticipated . . . that the distribution would disrupt school operations." Schools were also warned to provide procedures that would clearly tell students what kind of material must be submitted for approval and how it should be submitted and to "prescribe a definite brief period within which review of submitted material will be completed."

FUJISHIMA

Prior restraint of student expression in high schools continues to be controversial, and court decisions are not always consistent. In *Quarterman* v. *Byrd*,[18] the U.S. Court of Appeals for the Fourth Circuit agreed with the Second Circuit's decision in *Eisner,* that school officials could require prior submission of written material if an "expeditious review procedure" protects student rights. The Fifth Circuit Court of Appeals reached a similar conclusion in *Shanley* v. *Northeast Independent School District*.[19] But in *Fujishima* v. *Board of Education*,[20] the U.S. Court of Appeals for the Seventh Circuit disagreed, calling *Eisner* "unsound constitutional law."

The three plaintiffs in *Fujishima* were students at Lane Technical High School and Bowen High School in Chicago. For distributing an underground newspaper and anti-Vietnam war leaflets, they were suspended from school under the authority of section 6-19 of the rules of the Chicago Board of Education, which read: "No person shall be permitted . . . to distribute on the school premises any books, tracts, or other publications, . . . unless the same shall have been approved by the General Superintendent of Schools."

The Seventh Circuit court declared section 6-19 "unconstitutional as a prior restraint in violation of the First Amendment." The court said:

We believe the [Second Circuit] court erred in *Eisner* in interpreting *Tinker* to allow prior restraint of publication—long a constitutionally prohibited power—as a tool of school officials in forecasting substantial disruption of school activities.

Tinker, said the court, "is not a basis for establishing a system of censorship and licensing designed to *prevent* the exercise of First Amendment rights." The court enjoined Chicago school officials from enforcing section 6-19 but noted:

Such injunction will not prevent defendants from promulgating reasonable, specific regulations setting forth the time, manner and place in which the distribution of written materials may occur. . . . The board may then punish students who violate those regulations. Of course, the board may also establish a rule punishing students who publish and distribute on school grounds obscene or libelous literature.

DICKEY

While high school underground editors were arguing their cases in court, college journalists were not idle. The major college cases, however, involved school-sponsored publications.

The first important college case, *Dickey* v. *Alabama State Board of Education,*[21] was decided in 1967, two years before *Tinker.* The decision was favorable to student editor Dickey, but it was later declared moot because he decided not to reenroll at the college where he had been suspended. The case was significant, however, because it indicated the courts' desire to protect the rights of student journalists.

Gary Dickey was editor of the Troy State (Ala.) College student newspaper, the *Tropolitan,* in the spring of 1967 when Dr. Frank Rose, president of the University of Alabama, was attacked by state legislators for refusing to censor a student publication at the university's Montgomery campus. The publication in question, "Emphasis 67, A World in Revolution," was a program for a series of talks held at the university and contained excerpts from speeches by revolutionaries.

Although the controversy did not involve a publication at his college, Dickey wrote an editorial supporting Dr. Rose's refusal to censor "Emphasis 67" and condemning the "misinterpretation of the Emphasis program by members of the legislature,

and the considerable harassment they have caused Dr. Rose."
He showed the editorial to the *Tropolitan*'s faculty adviser and
the president of the college, and both told him not to publish
it. Dickey then left a blank space on the editorial page of the
newspaper but inserted the word "Censored" across the space
where the editorial normally would have appeared. He also
mailed the editorial to a Montgomery newspaper.

During the summer Dickey was refused readmission to Troy
State because of his "willful and deliberate insubordination."
The basis of the action taken against Dickey was a rule instituted
by Dr. Ralph Adams, president of Troy State, that there could
be no criticism in the *Tropolitan* of the governor or the state
legislature. Adams believed that a newspaper could not criticize
its "owners," in this case the governor and members of the legislature. Dickey contested the rule, and a U.S. District Court
decided in his favor, finding that the "no criticism" rule at Troy
State "violates the basic principles of academic and political expression as guaranteed by our Constitution." The court noted
that

> the establishment of an education program requires cer-
> tain rules and regulations necessary for maintaining an
> orderly program and operating the institution in a manner
> conducive to learning. However, the school and school
> officials have always been bound by the requirement that
> the rules and regulations *must be reasonable.* . . . Regu-
> lations and rules which are necessary in maintaining order
> and discipline are always considered reasonable. In the
> case now before this Court, it is clear that the maintenance
> of order and discipline of the students attending Troy State
> College had nothing to do with the rule that was invoked
> against Dickey.

The court also ruled that the school could not punish
Dickey "by cloaking his expulsion or suspension in the robe of
'insubordination.' " The court did note, however, that Troy
State had no legal obligation to permit Dickey to continue as
editor of the newspaper.

Troy State was ordered to readmit Dickey, but he decided
to enroll at Auburn University.

ANTONELLI

In a 1970 case a U.S. District Court in Massachusetts ruled
in *Antonelli* v. *Hammond*[22] that a college president could not

impose arbitrary restrictions on what may be communicated in a campus newspaper.

John Antonelli, editor of the *Cycle* at Fitchburg (Mass.) State College, submitted an article titled "Black Moochie" to the printer of the paper. The article, written by Eldridge Cleaver, had originally appeared in *Ramparts* magazine. It contained several four-letter words, and the printer refused to set it in type. Fitchburg President James J. Hammond agreed with the printer, calling the material "garbage." He told Antonelli he would refuse to allocate money for future editions of the *Cycle* unless he (Hammond) or someone acting with his authority approved the newspaper's contents. He then created an advisory board to examine contents of each issue of the *Cycle* prior to publication.

After disputes with the advisory board, Antonelli and other members of the editorial board submitted their resignations and Antonelli brought suit, contending that Hammond's action was a violation of First and Fourteenth Amendment press freedom guarantees.

The court found for the plaintiff. Judge W. Arthur Garrity noted that the advisory board was created to suppress obscene writings, and obscenity is not constitutionally protected. However, the powers of the advisory board were virtually unlimited and "could presumably be used, without change in form or need for expansion, to achieve complete control of the content of the newspaper." Also, no procedural safeguards had been established. "The advisory board bears no burden other than exercising its judgment; there is no appeal within the system from any particular decision; and there is no provision for prompt final judicial determination." Hence the establishment of the advisory board was held to be "an unconstitutional exercise of state power." Garrity also questioned whether obscenity in a college newspaper would be so "significantly disruptive of an orderly and disciplined educational process" as to meet the requirements for suppression of student expression set forth in *Tinker* (see Chapter 3).

An important issue in the case was the power of the college administration to withhold student activity funds from the newspaper. Garrity ruled that under Massachusetts law, once a determination had been made on how the funds were to be distributed, the expenditure was mandatory and that Hammond had no duty under the law "to ratify or to pass judgment on any particular activity."

The decision did state that reasonable restrictions may be

applied to the campus press. "For example, it may be lawful in the interest of providing students with the opportunity to develop their own writing and journalistic skills, to restrict publication in a campus newspaper to articles written by students. . . . But to tell a student what thoughts he may communicate is another matter." Because of the potentially great social value of a free student press, "it would be inconsistent with the basic assumptions of First Amendment freedoms to permit a campus newspaper to be simply a vehicle for ideas the state or the college administration deems appropriate."

PANARELLA

In a similar 1971 case, *Panarella* v. *Birenbaum*,[23] a New York State appeals court directed two college presidents not to interfere with the publication of attacks against religion. The presidents had threatened to suppress such articles in the Staten Island Community College *Dolphin* and the Richmond College *Times* after the *Dolphin* published an article described as a "scathing attack on the Catholic Church" and the *Times* printed an article considered "blasphemous" to Christianity. The court noted that with regard to religion the state must maintain "a strict neutrality," and these college newspapers were being used as "a forum for the free expression" of student opinions. The court decided that in this case there was no threat to the operation of the colleges.

TRUJILLO

In *Trujillo* v. *Love*,[24] a U.S. District Court in Colorado ruled that a student editor's suspension from a college newspaper for failure to follow her faculty adviser's vague restrictions on "controversial" writings abridged the student's First Amendment rights.

The problem arose when Southern Colorado State College decided to take over financial support of the college newspaper, the *Arrow*, and use the paper as an "instructional tool." Prior to July 1970 the newspaper had been a student enterprise financed by student activity fees, with no direct or indirect controls over student writings. After that date the mass communication department at the college started to supervise the newspaper.

The *Arrow*'s managing editor, Dorothy Trujillo, clashed twice with the paper's faculty adviser and the chairman of the mass communication department. On one occasion an editorial cartoon and caption were eliminated from an issue; on another an editorial which referred to a local municipal judge as a "small town farmer" was revised under pressure from the adviser. Miss Trujillo was then suspended from her duties and brought suit, charging that the "censoring" of her writings and her suspension from the paper were unconstitutional under the First Amendment.

The plaintiff testified that she knew she was supposed to submit "controversial" writings for clearance, but she did not know what "controversial" meant and the college furnished no guidelines to help define the word. The faculty adviser confirmed that he had made no effort to define "controversial."

The court decided in the plaintiff's favor, ruling that while the college could change the function of the paper, the change should have been made with more clarity and consistency:

> The idea of the policy change . . . was to prepare students through supervised *Arrow* work for a career in journalism. Yet student writing was not supervised. No advice or help was extended to *Arrow* staff either directly or in journalism classes. No standards were promulgated until after [one issue] had been unilaterally altered and even then staff members were only put on warning that they must secure approval for "controversial" material.

The court said that the adviser's conduct "had the effect of reining in on the writings of [one student] while leaving the work of other *Arrow* staff members unexpurgated." Furthermore, the term "controversial" was too vague. "Nor can we uphold such conduct merely because it comes labeled as 'teaching' when in fact little or no teaching took place."

Miss Trujillo sought a declaratory judgment that her rights had been violated, and the court granted her request. The court also ordered her reinstated to her position as managing editor, with back pay.

NEW LEFT EDUCATION PROJECT

Schools possess the authority to establish "reasonable regulations concerning the time, exact place in school, and the manner of distribution [of student periodicals]."[25] When officials make it difficult for students to distribute underground newspapers on high school grounds, staffs often resort to distribution on public sidewalks. Many college underground newspapers are distributed on campus without much difficulty. College administrators some-times fear that restrictive distribution rules "would only prove the suppression the paper's editorials inveigh against."[26]

An exception was the University of Texas, which not only restricted newspaper sales to designated areas but also required that they be sold only through vending machines. When the university's rules collided with the distribution plans of an under-ground newspaper, the editors of the paper sought relief in court.[27]

In February 1970 a U.S. District Court judge upheld the university's solicitation rules as "reasonable regulations of cam-pus conduct" and not discriminatory nor in violation of press freedom guarantees. Seven months later a three-judge federal panel ruled in favor of the *Rag,* the underground newspaper. The panel found the university's rules to be "unconstitutionally overbroad" and too dependent on "the will of the administrator." The university appealed the decision to the Supreme Court, and the case was sent back to the district court because of a procedural error.[28]

CHANNING CLUB

Another 1970 Texas case, *Channing Club* v. *Board of Regents of Texas Tech University,*[29] indicates that a college or university may not discriminate against a publication simply because it is produced by students.

Texas Tech had banned from the campus an issue of the *Catalyst,* an independently produced newspaper, partially on the basis that it had no literary merit and used objectionable lan-guage. The plaintiffs asked for injunctive relief, alleging that "since the University authorized [an] uninterrupted sale of news-papers, magazines and books . . . the action of Defendants sub-jected them to capricious and arbitrary treatment." Channing Club offered into evidence commercial publications sold on cam-pus that contained the same language Texas Tech had found objectionable in the *Catalyst.*

A U.S. District Court agreed with the plaintiffs that Texas Tech had been guilty of discrimination:

> There . . . being no legal distinction between the types of publications, the State does not become privileged to ban a publication merely because it is edited and published by students. . . . Plaintiffs may sell and distribute Issue 6,

Volume 1 of the *Catalyst* in the same manner and at the same times and places in which it was formerly distributed and sold.

HIGH SCHOOL STUDENTS DIFFERENTIATED

That high school students may not have the same rights of free expression as college students is indicated by *Schwartz* v. *Schuker*[30] and *Katz* v. *McAulay*.[31]

In *Schwartz* a U.S. District Court upheld a New York high school's expulsion of a student for distributing copies of an underground newspaper. The newspaper was critical of school officials and contained profanity. The court ruled:

> [T]he activities of high school students do not always fall within the same category as the conduct of college students, the former being in a much more adolescent and immature stage of life and less able to screen facts from propaganda.

Katz dealt with the right of high school students to distribute leaflets on school grounds asking for funds to help defend the "Chicago Eight." Their high school prohibited all solicitations except those for the Junior Red Cross.

The U.S. Court of Appeals for the Second Circuit found for the school and said:

> [A] state may decide that the appropriate discipline which requires the restriction of certain communicative actions may differ in the cases of university students from that called for in the cases of the younger secondary school pupils in relatively similar circumstances.

NONSTUDENTS

Nonstudents who distribute written materials on high school grounds without permission are not able to claim the protection of the principles enunciated in *Tinker*, a Washington court ruled in *State* v. *Owen*.[32]

The defendants, who were distributing draft literature, were arrested under the authority of a Washington statute which declared that nonstudents who loiter around school buildings without a lawful purpose are guilty of vagrancy. The defense charged that the law was an impermissible prior restraint on the free expression principles set forth in *Tinker,* but the Washington Supreme Court decided that *Tinker* dealt only with the rights of students and upheld the constitutionality of the statute.

NORTON

Courts have never clearly defined "reasonable rules" or what constitutes "material and substantial interference with school operations." Neither have they clearly indicated the extent of the burden school officials have when they attempt to justify a fore-cast of disruption or interference. Robert Trager, an authority on school press law, believes that in general school officials "must be able to conclusively prove that serious disruption would have occurred upon publication for courts to uphold any form of prior censorship."[33] In one case involving student leafleting, however, college officials were able to justify the suppression of student expression without such conclusive proof.

The case, *Norton* v. *Discipline Committee of East Tennessee State University,*[34] involved eight students who were suspended for distributing leaflets urging the student body to "stand up and fight" and "assault the bastions of university tyranny." When the students brought suit, both a U.S. District Court and the U.S. Court of Appeals for the Sixth Circuit upheld the right of college officials to "nip in the bud" disturbances they had forecast, even though there were no disturbances when the leaflets were dis-tributed.

Twenty-five students had warned the school to "get rid of this group of agitators," and one dean told the district court: "While some of these things we can never prove, in our hearts we know something like that [a disturbance] is just about to happen."

The court of appeals ruled that under *Tinker*

> [i]t is not required that the college authorities delay action against the inciters until after the riot has started and buildings have been taken over and damaged. The college authorities had the right to nip such action in the bud and prevent it in its inception. This is authorized even in criminal cases.

The decision prompted the American Civil Liberties Union to petition the Supreme Court, asking for a clarification of the standards set forth in the *Tinker* case. The ACLU contended that the material and substantial interference test had been "perverted" and asked that the Supreme Court apply the "clear and present danger" test to such cases (that freedom of speech or the press on college campuses not be suppressed unless there is a clear and present danger to the school). The ACLU also pointed out that *Tinker* left open the question of whether a student's expression could be restrained because of an anticipated disorderly reaction on the part of other students.[35]

PRIVATE SCHOOLS

Are private schools under the same legal obligation as public schools to allow at least limited freedom of the press on their campuses? Most authorities say no. The extension of press freedom to the campus rests on the reasoning that public schools are agencies of the state, and their officials are charged with upholding the Fifth and Fourteenth Amendment "due process" rights of students. The Fourteenth Amendment to the Constitution says that no state may abridge the rights of citizens without due process of law, and courts have interpreted this to include the rights of students to freedom of expression. It is difficult to apply the Fourteenth Amendment to private schools, however, because their officials are not state agents.[36] Until legal decisions clarify the free expression rights of private school students, they seem to have no legal right to freedom of the press on campus. Off campus, of course, they have the same rights as public school students.

ADVISER RESPONSIBILITY

When a high school publication is written and edited during school time and in the school building, the National Scholastic Press Association believes "censorship and control under these conditions . . . does not seem to infringe on freedom of the press."[37] A 1970 Wyoming case, *Jergeson* v. *Board of Trustees of School District No. 7*,[38] supports the assumption that faculty advisers to high school publications have a duty to censor if necessary, and failure to effectively control publication content can be considered in dismissal proceedings against the teacher.

Jergeson, a journalism instructor and adviser to the student newspaper, was dismissed from his job at Sheridan High School, partially on the basis of "[i]ncompetency, as evidenced by the

April 1, 1969, edition of . . . the school newspaper." The school board had taken exception to a photograph and an article and letter to the editor critical of school officials.

Jergeson maintained there were no rules and regulations concerning his responsibilities as adviser and the student editor was responsible for the publication. The board and the principal argued that Jergeson "was responsible for those who work on the paper and the production of the paper."

A Wyoming court upheld Jergeson's dismissal. The court observed:

> [Other incidents and] his apparent approval of a picture of a row of urinals in the school newspaper are not exactly fine examples to set for impressionable students. It is not that these students or at least a part of them have not been exposed to a more base and filthy humor outside the schools but in the halls of an institution where lofty ideals and examples should be the rule, it is out of place.

The court decided that the article and letter to the editor critical of faculty members (the details of which were not revealed in the decision) "collide with the rights of others, namely the teachers and administrators of the school." The court reasoned:

> The School Board could have well decided within its discretion that when the faculty member in charge of the [newspaper] . . . permits such articles to appear that he is in this way expressing his incompetence.
> The students in speaking out in the school paper as they did were not entertaining a subject such as the war in Vietnam or some controversial matter of a public nature but were making personal attacks on members of the faculty. . . . The school board could well be justified in deciding that this is a demonstration in poor journalism, one of the subjects taught by Mr. Jergeson and another example of his incompetency.

STAYING OUT OF COURT

Most censorship problems never reach the courts. Robert Trager has noted that "students and teachers generally comply with instructions rather than risk their student or professional positions."[39] High school censorship cases generally have dealt with underground newspapers. Greater freedom is allowed in colleges because students are older and the tradition of free expression is better established in institutions of higher learning than in secondary schools, and few college journalists get mad enough to take their troubles to court.

Moreover, court cases are time-consuming, expensive, and hard on the nerves. Each case must be decided on its own merits, and the outcome of a case is often hard to predict. "First Amendment rights must be balanced against the duty and obligation of the state to educate students in an orderly and decent manner to protect the rights not of a few but all of the students in the school system," a U.S. District Court has emphasized.[40] The decisions discussed in this chapter (and others to be discussed in subsequent chapters) show that the courts are concerned about student rights of free expression. But the law also recognizes that a public school needs reasonable rules in order to operate successfully, and the courts hesitate to interfere unless the rules clearly infringe on constitutional guarantees. Even the American Civil Liberties Union has advised students to avoid lengthy legal battles when their purposes can be accomplished by other means (the ACLU has furnished attorneys for many of the students who challenged school authorities).[41]

Also, censorship can take many forms, and some of the procedures used are not easily challenged in court. Printers sometimes refuse to set four-letter words in type (see Chapter 3). Advisers, administrators, publications boards, and student governments can be involved in "hidden censorship" when they withhold or manipulate allocations, choose "safe" editors, praise or condemn editorial stands. Such "hidden censorship" is often the biggest complaint of students.[42]

Students and faculty could avoid many conflicts if they could agree on guidelines for the student press and if students were involved in deciding important questions connected with the operation of student publications. Although the courts require only "reasonable" rules and not necessarily student participation in boards of publications, some problems might be solved without legal action if students were brought into the decision-making process.

Policy guidelines for student publications have not been universally adopted, even in colleges. A 1965 study of 65 college newspapers showed that staff members had to rely on such diverse guides as bylaws, constitutions, articles of incorporation, codes of ethics, statements of principles, handbooks, manuals, style books, policy statements, and notes from college officials. The length of such documents ranged from two to seventy pages. Eighteen percent of the colleges had no policy guidelines at all.[43] There is no evidence to indicate that the situation has improved since that time. Linda Gregory, who studied 222 Indiana high school newspapers for her 1971 master's thesis at Indiana University, found that fewer than half of them had codes of ethics or policy statements to guide student staff members.[44]

In calling for the adoption of "explicit" guidelines for college publications, Annette Gibbs suggests that they "show no evidence of discrimination, deprival of due process, or arbitrary or capricious action." She also believes that guidelines should deal not only with legal questions but also with the functions of the publications and the ethics and obligations of student journalists.[45] Robert Trager and Ron Ostman have proposed comprehensive model guidelines for high school publications, including detailed suggestions for meaningful student participation in a board of publications.[46]

The National Association of Secondary School Principals recommends that guidelines of at least a general nature be established for high school students. These guidelines should categorize material that is "libelous, obscene, scandalous, or clearly provocative as unacceptable." Furthermore,

> [i]t may well be necessary for principals to insist upon the right of distribution, or prior review, to ensure that they have an opportunity to make this judgment. To avoid unnecessary legal confrontation, suspension, and/or disruption, school regulations should provide for the appeal of the principal's decision leading to final determination by the [school] board. This would afford the board more participation in case-by-case process. It would also avoid throwing an impasse immediately over to the courts and assist in achieving uniformity within a particular school district.[47]

The American Bar Association recommends that schools consider some "right of reply" rules:

> When the student press is supported by compulsory student fees or other significant . . . subsidy or where there is a generally accepted public identification with the particular institution, it may properly be subject to rules providing for a right of reply by any person adversely treated in its

publication or in disagreement with its editorial policy or its treatment of a given event.[48]

A policy that might be considered is the use of a disclaimer on the editorial pages of student publications similar to the one that appears in the *Philosopher* of Lew Wallace High School in Gary, Indiana:

> The Philosopher is published by Journalism students of Lew Wallace High School. The opinions are those of the writers and not necessarily those of the school administration or faculty.

A committee appointed to study operations of the University of South Carolina *Gamecock* recommended going a step further. The committee suggested that the newspaper make it clear that its contents do not necessarily reflect the views of the university, the student body, or even all student staff members.[49] While such disclaimers are more for public relations than legal reasons, they could result in looser controls over student opinion.

UNDERGROUND NEWSPAPERS

Guidelines for the distribution of underground newspapers written, edited, and published outside school grounds are difficult to establish. The Maryland State Board of Education decided on the following policy with regard to student publications produced without school sponsorship:

> It is the opinion of this Board that in the several senior high schools in this State, a Review Board must be established whose membership may consist of faculty and students but in no event shall the student membership fall below fifty percent of the total membership of said Review Board. The student members of said Review Board shall be determined by the student body through the Student Council or any similar method. At the outset, said Review Board must establish guidelines by which all student publications must conform. All such student publications must be submitted to the Review Board within a reasonable time *after* its [sic] dissemination [as established by said Review Board]. Only the Principal or other designated school officials will have the power to determine what, if any, punitive measures may be taken in the case of violation of said guidelines.

In the case of the middle or junior high school [grades 7 and 8 and 9 where applicable], the rules, as stated above, would be identical except [as established by said Review Board] prior to dissemination of such publications.

In the case of the Primary School [grades K through 6] the school administration shall continue to have absolute authority on dissemination of any student publication. It is hoped that even at this level, the school authorities will allow some latitude in allowing primary school pupils the opportunity of free expression in their publications where such is deemed proper.

In all cases, the School administration shall have emergency powers where dissemination of any student document would present a potentially dangerous or disruptive situation in a school.[50]

Students who desire fewer controls over their publications might consider the words of Lester G. Benz, executive secretary of the Quill and Scroll Society:

With more freedom comes greater responsibility. But freedom must be earned and deserved. Failure of student journalists to recognize this relationship inevitably leads to censorship and places both administrator and adviser in a position where administrative control becomes necessary and censorship may be the only answer.[51]

SUMMARY

Student rights of free expression must be balanced with the need of school officials to maintain order. Public high schools and colleges are allowed "reasonable" rules regarding the publication and distribution of the student press; however, they may not suppress student expression unless there is "material and substantial interference" with school operations. What constitutes such interference is still being defined by the courts; hence decisions may not always be consistent. However, this interference must be something more than "discomfort and unpleasantness."

Courts are concerned with student rights of due process, so school officials should make provisions for intraschool appeal of an administrator's ruling. School rules should clearly define what kind of material is prohibited, how questionable material must be submitted for approval, and to whom. A speedy decision must be reached.

When a student publication is produced during school time and in the school building, censorship and control do not seem to infringe on freedom of the press.

To avoid conflicts, students and faculty should jointly decide on guidelines for the publication and distribution of all student periodicals, both school-sponsored and "underground."

CHAPTER TWO

LIBEL

HIGH SCHOOL AND COLLEGE ADMINISTRATORS do a lot of worrying about the dangers of libel (defamation of character) in the campus press. The possibility that student journalists might involve themselves and others in a libel suit is one of the major justifications for tight controls over student publications. "Certainly the student press can injure reputation as easily as its independent cousin downtown," points out John C. Merrill. "But who is in the position to pay damages which might be incurred by a student operating in a 'free press' campus situation? Certainly not the student editor."[1]

Despite the fears of school officials, libel judgments against university and high school presses are rare. A survey for the University of California in 1969 failed to turn up "a single case of libel judgment against a college or university newspaper or against a college or university."[2] The research for this book uncovered only one judgment against a school district for libel in a student publication.

Vernon W. Smith explains why libel suits involving the student press are not numerous:

> Legal action is time consuming and many of the individuals who might otherwise sue for libel are employed by the institution which bears the legal responsibility for what the publication does. When the desire is to punish the person committing the libel, there are other methods more easily used than the courts. Many cases are settled out of court with or without initiation of court action. In most cases, the institution possesses means of punitive action which do not require court action and its attendant publicity.[3]

Nevertheless, libel suits have been filed as a result of student writing, as the following cases illustrate. Even though most have been settled out of court or dropped, they have created problems for the defendants. And as student journalists enjoy more freedom of expression, the possibilities for libel increase. "It doesn't take much imagination to speculate on the number of potential libel cases circulating in campus journalism today," remarks John Behrens.[4]

SOVEREIGN IMMUNITY

One reason the student press is not commonly sued for libel is that public high schools and colleges in many states are immune from such suits under the doctrine of "sovereign immunity." This common-law rule holds that institutions of learning, as agencies of the state, are not liable for the torts (civil wrongs) of their officers, agents, and employees in the absence of a statute making them liable.

State immunity from tort liability has largely been terminated by statute in Iowa, New York, Oregon, Utah, and Washington and partially repudiated by court decisions in Alaska, Arizona, Arkansas, California, District of Columbia, Florida, Idaho, Illinois, Indiana, Kentucky, Michigan, Minnesota, Nebraska, Nevada, New Jersey, Rhode Island, and Wisconsin. School districts specifically have been held liable for the torts of their agents in Arizona, Illinois, Minnesota, and Wisconsin.[5]

However, in many states institutional liability in a libel suit is uncertain at best.

CHARITABLE IMMUNITY

Private schools are not protected by sovereign immunity but in some states may be able to claim "charitable immunity" from tort liability. Charitable institutions (those maintained not for profit, gain, or advantage) have claimed such protection under common law because of their limited financial means and the reluctance of courts to destroy a charitable trust. However, the rule of charitable immunity is not well settled in all jurisdictions, and its usefulness in a libel suit is questionable. For example, in some tort actions courts have reasoned that injured parties not being benefited by the charity at the time of injury can sue charitable institutions for damages.[6]

SEPARATE CORPORATIONS

Some colleges and universities encourage separate incorporation of their student newspapers and other publications in hopes that such incorporation will provide some protection against libel action. But Thomas Blackwell warns that "there is always uncertainty as to the extent to which the courts will respect the legal fiction of separate corporate identity in the event of suit, if the parent corporation continues to exercise any substantial degree of control over the subsidiary."[7]

What is "substantial degree of control" is open to debate. However, Vanderbilt University was excused as defendant in a libel suit when school officials argued successfully that a student newspaper was not a university publication. Vanderbilt presented evidence that there was no advance censorship of the newspaper, no member of the university staff was assigned to it as an adviser, students made their own contracts with printers and handled other business affairs, and profits or losses belonged to the editor and business manager.[8]

ADVISERS AND ADMINISTRATORS

The doctrines of sovereign and charitable immunity do not usually extend to school employees. As a general rule they are liable for torts arising out of their own negligence. Some schools indemnify employees who suffer losses in a civil action in connection with their duties; in others the possibility exists that an adviser or administrator might have to pay damages out of his own pocket if a libel judgment is entered against him. All those who take part in the publication of a libel are responsible for it. R. W. Tudor emphasizes that "any person who presumably could have stopped publication of the libelous matter and failed to do so is liable."[9]

Those who play a "secondary part" in the dissemination of information published by another may escape liability by showing that they had no reason to believe that actionable libel was being committed, but the burden of proof is on the defendant. Librarians and news vendors, for example, have escaped liability on these grounds,[10] but it is doubtful that advisers and administrators could be placed in the same category. However, the relationship between the parties involved can be a factor in cases involving tort liability,[11] so it might be argued that a high school adviser who regularly reads all copy prior to publication runs a greater risk in a libel suit than a college adviser who normally does not. It could be argued that a principal or administrator who does not pass on the acceptability of copy might be excused as a defendant on these grounds.

Foreseeability is an important part of negligence cases, and M. Chester Nolte and John Phillip Linn warn: "If there is a known hazard, the teacher is expected to instruct the students thoroughly as to the dangers involved. Failure to furnish ordinary precautionary instruction constitutes negligence on the part of the teacher."[12]

STUDENTS

A staff member of a student publication may be legally responsible for his torts, even if he is a minor. However,

in the case of negligence, children have been recognized as a special group to whom a more or less subjective standard of conduct is to be applied, which may vary according to age, intelligence, and experience, so that in some cases immunity may be conferred in effect by finding merely that there is no negligence.[13]

The tort expert, William Prosser, cites only three cases in which minors were found responsible for defamation; they date from 1835 to 1910, and apparently none of them involved schools.[14] Moreover, a minor may be responsible for his torts but his parents are not always legally responsible for their child's misdeeds. Parents are responsible if they consented to the child's act or failed to control their offspring. In other situations their liability is questionable.

So what it boils down to is that the institution may have the financial resources to pay large damages but may be immune from tort action. Advisers, administrators, and students may not be immune but perhaps do not have the financial resources to pay meaningful damages. Faced with these considerations, many persons who believe they have been libeled by a student publication decide not to sue.

COLORADO

A controversy at the University of Colorado showed that a possible libel can cause plenty of trouble for school officials and student journalists, even though no suit is filed. In September 1962 a weekly supplement to the Colorado *Daily* carried an essay which referred to Senator Barry Goldwater as "a fool, a mountebank, a murder [*sic*], no better than a common criminal." After the commercial press picked up the story, Colorado President Quigg Newton, the Board of Regents, the university's Board of Publications, and *Daily* editor Gary Althen all sent apologies to Goldwater. The publications board informed Althen that he had been guilty of printing libel but voted not to fire him. Only Carl Mitcham, the student who wrote the essay, stood firm. He challenged Goldwater to sue him.

Goldwater then wrote Newton, questioning whether the university president knew or cared about what was going on. "To put it briefly, I doubt if you have the interest or concern to be in the position you hold," the Arizona senator wrote. Newton answered: "We have a genuine democracy of ideas on campus . . . I shall not silence them."

Althen then printed a letter to the editor, also written by Mitcham, which made several derogatory comments about political figures, including an observation that former President Eisenhower was an "old futzer." This was too much for Newton. He asked the Board of Publications to fire Althen. "There is no defense for students in responsible positions who mistakenly assume that academic freedom and freedom of speech are unlimited licenses to indulge in vilification and personal abuse," Newton told the board. However, the board refused to fire the editor, and Althen would not resign. So Newton fired Althen by executive authority and added three faculty members to the Board of Publications.

Newton justified his action on the grounds that Althen "displayed a pattern of editorial irresponsibility that required his removal." (Althen had also printed editorials favoring Red China's admission to the United Nations and asking that big-time football be abandoned at Colorado. Both had caused minor furors.) Newton told the student body: "The fundamental motive of my actions in this case is to protect your academic freedoms, not diminish them. I want more student participation in University administration, not less. But I want it in the hands of responsible students, and so must you." Newton's critics maintained that Althen had been fired "not because the campus thought the editor had sinned, but because the newspapers and politicians outside the campus had thought so."[15]

PACIFIC

In 1968 an editorial critical of a university health service and a campus physician cost a college editor his position. The editorial was printed in the *Index,* the student newspaper at small (1,200 students) Pacific University in Forest Grove, Oregon. The director of health service at the university thought he had been libeled and filed suit against the dean of students, the provost, the university president, the student writer, and the student body, asking $50,000 damages. The *Index* published a retraction, the student writer was removed from the newspaper's staff after apologizing to the physician, and the editor of the *Index* resigned. The doctor then dropped the suit.

Pacific Dean of Students Charles Trombley believed that the retraction prompted the doctor to drop the matter: "This satisfied the doctor who felt that to ignore the issue would be bypassing an opportunity to educate those responsible."[16]

The Pacific case has two lessons for other student publications: (1) Be careful when writing about matters which might affect the reputation of a respected professional man. (2) Consider running a retraction if you have no solid legal defense. A retraction may satisfy an injured party and also may help to reduce damages if a suit is pursued successfully. To be on the safe side, consult an attorney about the wording of the retraction.

CALIFORNIA STATE

As a general rule, a retraction should be "full and fair" and withdraw any charges made against an individual. An assistant professor of English at California State College, Los Angeles, believed he was libeled by the college's newspaper and filed suit when the paper would not completely retract statements it made about him.

In the spring of 1964 Cal State's *College Times* was editorializing in favor of student evaluation of faculty teaching. Professor Philip Friedman was against this idea. He wrote an item for the paper's "Open Forum" feature; under the heading "Student's Job—Learning, Not Grading His Profs," Friedman called the *College Times'* proposals "abhorrent."

Two months later a *College Times* summer edition ran a letter to the editor from one "Ann Konrad," who described Friedman as "overbearing," "sarcastic," "a phoney," and the "most unpopular, disliked teacher in the department." Faculty members complained about the letter and the *Summer Times* ran the following apology:

> Last week's anonymous and unverified Open Forum column by "Ann Konrad" containing several unsubstantiated statements about Philip A. Friedman, asst. professor of English, was meant to show that students have no systematic means for evaluating teaching effectiveness of professors, not to injure the reputation of Professor Friedman. We express our regrets to Professor Friedman for our error in judgment.

Friedman was spending the summer in New York, but once back on campus he demanded a complete retraction. An October issue of the *College Times* carried this statement:

> An "Open Forum" column in the July 20 issue of SUMMER TIMES carried under the pseudonym of "Ann Konrad" attacked the teaching competence of Philip Friedman, asst. prof. of English.
>
> SUMMER TIMES editor Felix Gutierrez is not on the editorial staff of the COLLEGE TIMES and is therefore not in a position to offer a retraction.
>
> THE COLLEGE TIMES wishes to apologize for this "Ann Konrad" article which we feel exposed Professor Friedman to ridicule and contempt and was damaging to him professionally.

Friedman still was not satisfied. His attorney wrote the *College Times* demanding a complete retraction "to mitigate the severity of damages to his reputation." The retraction must clearly indicate that the statements "were, in their entirety, false."

The newspaper did not comply, and Friedman filed suit against *Summer Times* editor Gutierrez, "Ann Konrad," and the Associated Students of California State College of Los Angeles, among others, asking for a total of $200,000.

The defense centered around the fact that Friedman had provoked an attack through his "Open Forum" article, that he had suffered no real damages, that he had not demanded a retraction within the twenty-day limit stipulated in California law, and that, in any event, a retraction was printed.[17] The outcome of the case was not reported in the lawbooks.

VANDERBILT

When publications are sued for libel, they often rely on one or more of three defenses: truth, qualified privilege, and fair

comment and criticism. In most states, if the defendants can
prove that the statements made about the plaintiff are true, the
suit will not succeed. Qualified privilege allows a publication
to report official legislative, judicial, and governmental proceedings—even when these proceedings contain libelous statements—
as long as the reports are fair, accurate, and impartial. Journalists
may also fairly criticize what "public men" (authors, actors, etc.)
and institutions offer to society.

Qualified privilege was combined with another defense,
consent to the libel, in a case involving the *Hustler,* student newspaper at Vanderbilt University.[18]

In 1954 the Vanderbilt humor magazine, *Chase,* ran a
photograph of two-year-old Pamela Langford. The photo, with
the caption "Daughter Loves Mother," appeared in a Mother's
Day feature and, according to Pamela's father, implied that the
girl was amenable to acts of illicit sexual intercourse. He brought
suits for libel and invasion of privacy against the university,
asking for $180,000 in damages (see also Chapter 10).

The *Hustler* ran a story of the pleadings under the headline:

$180,000 SUIT FILED BY LOCAL MINISTER OVER CHASE PHOTO

CLAIMS ISSUE "LEWD, BAWD, VULGAR"

"SPREAD SEX, FILTH, SLIME AND SMUT"

Langford objected to this coverage and filed new suits against
the student newspaper. But a Tennessee court dismissed the
case, partially on the grounds that Langford had cooperated with
Hustler reporters and sought publicity. The court said:

> All the evidence shows that plaintiff Mr. Langford
> told these two students [*Hustler* reporters] he wanted pub-
> licity, referred them to his lawyers for the legal details, the
> lawyers advised them when the suits were filed, and they
> made a fair and accurate statement of the pleadings, giving
> the alleged defamatory parts in the plaintiff's own words.

IOWA STATE

The defense of fair comment and criticism is sometimes
thought to be a form of privilege and sometimes interpreted as
a separate legal rule. In 1971 the Iowa State *Daily* successfully
cited the "privilege of fair comment" when it was sued by
Campus Alliance, Inc., a student discount buying service.

Campus Alliance objected to *Daily* charges that it was a

"slipshod organization . . . whose business approaches are questionable" and took particular exception to a *Daily* editorial which read, in part:

> Following a Sept. 12 [1970] story in the Daily about CA, Campus Alliance representatives came to the Daily office to discuss their business. At the beginning of the discussion, the CA promoters re-stated that CA only received income from sales of the $3 discount cards. By the end of the meeting, the CA representatives admitted they were receiving money from participating merchants for a "progressive advertising plan." This plan amounts to little more than kickbacks or rebates.
> Such dishonesty has led us to doubt the professionalism and business ethics of CA.

Campus Alliance filed a $100,000 libel suit against the *Daily,* but an Iowa judge dismissed the action. His decision read, in part:

> This organization, its origin, its methods of its operation, were all matters of interest and concern to the students, faculty and staff at Iowa State University. . . . It is my conclusion that the articles were inspired for the purpose of disclosing to [Daily] readers the nature and operation of plaintiff's company and that defendant's motives were not due to ill will or spite and therefore privileged under the law.[19]

ARIZONA

In 1964 the U.S. Supreme Court's landmark decision in *New York Times* v. *Sullivan* (376 U.S. 254) greatly extended the allowable limits of comment where public officials are concerned. The Court noted that there is "a profound national commitment to the principle that debate on public issues should be uninhibited, robust, and wide-open, and that it may well include vehement, caustic, and sometimes unpleasantly sharp attacks on government and public officials." The Court decided that constitutional guarantees require a federal rule that public officials cannot recover for defamatory falsehoods relating to their official conduct unless the statements are made with "actual malice." Actual malice was defined as "knowledge that it [the statement] was false or . . . reckless disregard of whether it was false or not." After this ruling it became difficult for public officials to successfully sue commercial publications for libel.

Are campus journalists protected by this *"New York Times* rule"? *Klahr* v. *Winterble*[20] indicates that the *New York Times* rule may extend into campus politics, at least in colleges.

In November 1963 the University of Arizona *Wildcat* printed the following editorial on its front page:

THE DEMAGOGUE FROM TEMPE

Senator Gary Peter Klahr, the campus demagogue, is now hissing in another pit, we see.

His latest diatribe was at Tuesday's Senate appropriations board meeting. Klahr was elected to it last year as the final member, a gift of newly elected Student Senators who knew no better.

Tuesday he exposed a childish threat to attempt to hamstring the Wildcat by taking away its student subsidy.

For the reader's information, that subsidy amounts to about one-fifth of one per cent per copy of the Wildcat.

Klahr's latest demagoguery shows he means that if the Wildcat won't play ball with him and his ideas, that he wants no Wildcat.

History proves that this is a dictator's first move. Stalin, Hitler, and Mussolini first killed the free press to substitute a lackey press of their own.

Going along with that, Gary Peter Klahr has introduced a bill calling for a Senate Newsletter. Sound familiar? Well, he also wants to have editorial comment in that Newsletter.

He has often claimed that he has nothing but the interests of the dear old student body at heart.

As he did his undergraduate work at Tempe, we can hardly believe that he really means it down to the bottom of his genius.

He has managed to confound, confuse and overwhelm other Senators, largely by his 1,000-word-a-minute delivery. Even stalwarts throw up their hands, saying "enough, I agree," just to get him to stop, stop, stop.

Some persons say that the Senator was a child prodigy.

We have nothing against prodigies; maybe all Klahr needs is a bigger Mechano Set, but we're against buying him one.

The worst threat that this junior-grade demagogue poses is that by his gestures and screaming, he might outlast and so disgust real Senators that student government would crash down around our ears.

His ramblings and exhortations about the Wildcat and "the Administration" are but a continuation of his desire to see his name bandied about as a troublemaker and a fanatic.

Both of which he is.

By the way, Senator Klahr, which side of the stands
are you planning to sit on at the Tempe game?
OR DO YOU WANT TO TAKE AWAY THE ATH-
LETIC SUBSIDY, TOO?

Six months later student senator Klahr filed a $30,000 libel
suit against Peter Winterble, editor-in-chief of the newspaper,
and Professor Sherman Miller, adviser to the *Wildcat*. Klahr
claimed that the editorial had damaged his reputation and his
prospects of finding employment as an attorney in Arizona after
his graduation from law school. The defense maintained that
Klahr was a "public official" in the university community. A
superior court entered a summary judgment for the defendants
and Klahr appealed the ruling.

An Arizona Court of Appeals found for the defendants and
cited *Times* v. *Sullivan:*

> We believe the impact of the *New York Times* rule
> upon the libel law of the country and of this state to be
> such that, regardless of whether the rule be mandatory
> upon us in this case under the federal constitution, the
> rule should govern under the undisputed circumstances
> here. If this were a "play" government upon the campus
> of the University of Arizona [as Klahr had argued] then
> all participants in this litigation were engaged in the
> game. . . .
>   . . . we do not conceive that it would be appropriate
> that there be one law of libel in this state for "public offi-
> cials" off the campuses of our state universities and [that]
> another law of libel [should] be applicable to the student
> government officers upon such campuses, when the systems
> of politics and news media are so obviously patterned after
> the situation off campus, and when the publication is pri-
> marily addressed to the "interested community."

Despite the ruling in *Klahr*, student journalists still do not
know how far they can go when they criticize student "public
officials" or school administrators. Robert Trager points out
that student publications have never clearly been given the "non-
malicious reporting" privileges accorded the commercial press in
Times v. *Sullivan*. Even though most school administrators are
"public officials," student journalists must be careful, especially
in high schools, that their criticism is based on demonstrable facts
and will not cause interference with the operations of the school.
Trager sums up:

On college campuses, there is little doubt that student
publications can now constructively criticize school administrators. . . . In high schools, courts still consider the rela-
tive immaturity of the students to be a mitigating factor,
and criticism there must be less pointed.[21]

Clifton O. Lawhorne indicates that not all school administrators may be "public officials" within the meaning of the *New
York Times* rule. He says that the definition of public officials
as those who "have, or appear to have, substantial responsibility
for or control over the conduct of government affairs" is vague
enough so no uniformity may be expected in court decisions:
"Depending on the point of view, the public official rule of law
can be applied or rejected at the trial court level."[22]

While *Klahr* provides a precedent for those who might argue
that a student government officer at a college or university is a
"public official," there is no similar case in the high school area.
For example, is a high school student body president a "public
official" within the meaning of the *New York Times* rule? Dale
R. Spencer speculates that this is a possibility,[23] but without a
court decision speculation is all that is possible.

"UNNAMED UNIVERSITY"

In 1966 a U.S. Court of Appeals ruled in *Pauling* v. *Globe-
Democrat Publishing Co.* (362 F. 2d 188) that "public figures"
who project themselves into "the arena of public controversy"
are also bound by the *New York Times* rule. They, like public
officials, must plead and prove "actual malice" in order to recover for defamatory falsehoods. (The U.S. Supreme Court let the
decision stand.) Is a student leader at a university a "public
figure"?

This was one of the issues in a libel case at an unnamed
large state university where a black student leader claimed she
was defamed by a cartoon in the student newspaper. The student,
"Miss C," had been an unsuccessful candidate for student body
president at the university and after the election was a spokesman
for black students who were charging that the school's football
coach was guilty of racism. The cartoon showed a black woman
in Puritan dress trying to "crucify" the football coach. The
woman in the cartoon was not named, but on her dress were
initials identical to those of "Miss C."

"Miss C" brought a $30,000 libel suit against the editor of
the student newspaper, the cartoonist, and the State Board of

Education. She claimed she was identified in the cartoon "by certain grotesque exaggerations of her features and by her initials on the drawing" and that the cartoon "falsely, maliciously and in a libelous manner depicted her in a false, ridiculous and contemptible and derogatory situation."

The case never went to trial. The company which had insured the university against libel purchased "Miss C's" claim for a nominal sum (libel insurance companies often prefer settlement to costly and time-consuming litigation). However, had the case gone to trial, the defense was ready to argue that "Miss C" was a "public figure" within the university community.

Another interesting aspect of the case was the eventual inclusion of a news law teacher as a defendant. The teacher had exhibited the cartoon in question during a class discussion of the case and was charged with "republishing" the libel. Dennis O. Gray suggests that communication law teachers refrain from exhibiting possibly libelous materials which deal with a pending case, since "every republication of a libel is a fresh publication." Discussion of a pending case is allowable, but exhibition is risky.[24]

INDIANA

Recovery for defamation of character is limited, by and large, to individuals. A journalist may criticize a large group without being liable to the group as a whole or to individual members of the group. Only when the group is small enough so that individual members can show identification and personal defamation can a civil libel suit be successful.

At a student rally on the campus of Indiana University, a graduate student allegedly called the campus police force "ill trained" and "the dregs of society." The Indiana *Daily Student* published the quote, and thirty-seven campus policemen filed a $740,000 slander (oral defamation) suit against the graduate student and a $740,000 libel suit against the *Daily Student*. (It should be pointed out that simply because a newspaper quotes a source for a defamatory statement it is not protected. The law holds that "tale bearers are as bad as tale makers.")

Attorney Richard Cardwell, who defended the graduate student, filed a motion to dismiss, partially on the basis that the police force was too large to support the idea that any individual in the group had been defamed. The court dismissed both the slander and the libel suits because the plaintiffs did not have a case on the basis of their complaints.[25]

RUTGERS

Identification of policemen was also an issue in a 1971 case, *Scelfo* v. *Rutgers University*.[26]

The plaintiffs, two Newark mounted policemen, were assigned to the Rutgers campus during a 1968 confrontation between Students for a Democratic Society and Young Americans for Freedom. Their pictures appeared in the Rutgers student newspaper along with a student-written essay and a headline: "YAF's, Cops, Rightists: Racist Pig Bastards." The policemen brought suit for unspecified libel damages against the essayist, the newspaper's adviser, and the university.

A New Jersey court granted summary judgment for the defendants, noting that the word "pig" is not necessarily libelous on its face, and neither the police force nor the mounted police were called "racists" or "bastards" in the essay. Moreover, the policemen were not personally identified in either the article or the photograph. The court said:

> No reference is made in the body of [the] article to the photograph; no caption identifies the two men pictured as the specific mounted policemen mentioned [as pigs] . . . and the profile shots were taken at enough distance to render the individual features of the two men indiscernible.

The court also pointed out that policemen were public officials within the meaning of the *New York Times* rule, and their failure to plead and prove actual malice was another reason for dismissing the complaint. The decision read, in part:

> As mounted policemen of the Newark police force plaintiffs perform governmental duties directly related to the public interest and have, or appear to the public to have, substantial responsibility for or control over the conduct of governmental affairs. . . . The alleged defamatory statements . . . related to the discharge of official duties of patrolmen assigned to the demonstration.

OHIO

Most libel cases are civil suits in which the plaintiff seeks monetary compensation for damage to his reputation or professional standing. On rare occasions libel is treated as a crime, with prosecution by the government and the possiblity of a prison sentence if the accused is found guilty. Criminal libel is an offense against society and may involve expression that disrupts public order or maliciously defames the state and its officials.

A mimeographed flyer distributed to Ohio University students in 1969 resulted in a criminal libel charge against a former Ohio University coed. The flyer said that a municipal court judge and an Athens, Ohio, police captain comprised a "thug-racist" power structure and also accused the police captain of "trumping up" drug charges against university students. The defendant faced a possible prison sentence of one to five years, but the case was dismissed after she apologized to the parties involved.[27]

ARKANSAS

If there is no satisfactory defense to a libel suit, the defendants may be better off settling out of court for a nominal sum rather than fighting the suit.

A student editor of the *Razorback,* University of Arkansas yearbook, and a printing company were named defendants in a $25,000 libel suit filed by a *Razorback* staff member. An out-of-court settlement of $500 was arranged, half of which was paid by the editor's father and half by the printing company.

The suit arose as a result of the following paragraph which appeared in a section of the *Razorback* devoted to problems connected with the yearbook's preparation:

> And, of course, I spent the whole first semester tracing my favorite lush, [name], through George's [a local beer parlor] and his apartment, trying my best to get some authentic copy. . . . Speaking of people going, *The Razorback*'s sharpest alcoholic, [name], came about once and left.[28]

NEW YORK

Suits as a result of libel in high school publications are relatively rare. It is usually difficult to collect damages from a high school or a high school student, as the opening section of this chapter indicates. And high school publications are more carefully controlled than the college press.

Nevertheless, libel suits have been filed, with yearbook content often the reason. An example is a suit brought by a New York high school girl in 1962.

A caption under the photograph of 16-year-old Irene Bickerton in the 1962 *Pacer,* the yearbook of the Sanford H. Calhoun High School in Merrick (N.Y.) read:

A soft, meek, patient, humble, tranquil spirit . . . THOMAS
DEKKER—"The Honest Whore."

The line was from a Dekker play written in 1604. About
500 copies of the yearbook were distributed, but a school official
said that half of them were recalled and the caption was changed
to:

Gentle of speech, beneficent of mind . . . HOMER—"Odys-
sey."

Nevertheless, Miss Bickerton filed suit, contending that the
"meanings specifically intended to be conveyed [in the original
caption] were vicious, insidious, and calculated to injure and
were the meanings which naturally would be given . . . and
were given by persons who read them." She sought damages of
$750,000; other members of her family asked for $250,000 more.
Defendants were the Board of Education, the principal of the
high school, and a yearbook printing company. The suit was
settled out of court.[29]

NEW JERSEY
Another yearbook caption resulted in a $38,000 libel judg-
ment against the South Orange-Maplewood (N.J.) Board of Education, adviser-teacher Robert Cuddy, and the American Yearbook Company in 1970.[30]
The caption, containing a double entendre ("A good fisher-
man and a master baiter"), appeared under the photograph of a
ninth-grader in the 1966 yearbook of South Orange Junior High
School. Over 300 copies of the book were distributed.
A county court jury in Newark deliberated for three hours,
following a six-day trial, before bringing in a verdict for the
plaintiff. He was awarded $11,000 for damage to his reputation
and $27,000 for mental suffering. It was believed to be the first
libel judgment against a school board in New Jersey history and
the first successful libel case in the country involving the contents
of a school yearbook.[31]
The judgment was against all three defendants, but whether
adviser Cuddy had to pay damages is unclear. In the past, New
Jersey has "saved harmless" school district employees in negligence cases under the principle that "a master and servant or
principal and agent shall be considered a single tortfeasor." Other

states that "save harmless" school employees in negligence cases include California, Connecticut, Massachusetts, Minnesota, New York, and Wyoming.[32] In most of these states, school districts pay any judgment entered against an agent.

OREGON

School officials usually are responsible for student "publications" in any form—printing, tape recordings, films, kinescopes, radio, and television. In 1970 a film made by two students in a Deschutes, Oregon, high school resulted in a libel suit.

The film, reportedly titled "Sick America," was produced for an honors English class. It allegedly showed an automobile sales manager discussing a business transaction with a teen-age girl, while a record suggestive of narcotics use played in the background.

The sales manager contended that he was depicted as an unscrupulous car salesman and wrongly identified as having sold narcotics. He filed suit against the school district and five teachers, asking $200,000 in punitive damages and $50,000 in general damages for each of the four times the film was shown to a high school class. The students who made the film were not named as defendants. The plaintiff said: "The teachers knew that the words and pictures and meanings were false." The school district carried liability insurance and the teachers were also covered by policies carried through a teachers' organization.[33]

LIBEL INSURANCE

Schools normally can purchase libel insurance to cover their employees and agents. Such coverage usually is included in blanket tort liability policies. As a general rule, the voluntary procurement of liability insurance by a school does not waive its immunity from suit but may limit its liability to the amount of the policy.[34] If there is a question of whether public money can be expended to purchase liability insurance for school employees and agents, administrators and teachers can often purchase insurance through an educational organization.

If possible, those connected with school publications should be covered by such insurance, especially in colleges. Dennis O. Gray suggests:

Perhaps the first thing that teachers and student editors should do, to allay their fears, is to check with the administration to determine if the university carries a personal liability policy covering school employees who may be charged with libel, slander, deprivation of civil rights, and other torts. In this day and age the university should carry a minimum $200,000 personal liability policy on all staff members, employees and agents.[35]

The Board of Trustees at Indiana University recently provided financial support for administrators, faculty advisers, and salaried staff members of student publications who may become involved in libel suits. The trustees' action of May 1971 was made possible by legislation passed by the Indiana legislature. Indemnity is limited to reasonable costs and expenses in connection with a case and any amount "for which such person becomes liable by reason of any judgment."[36]

High school advisers and administrators should also be protected. Kern Alexander predicts "a greater volume of tort cases against employees and school districts" in the years ahead due to a decline in the reliance on the sovereign immunity doctrine and students' increased knowledge of their legal rights.[37]

AVOIDING LIBEL

Whether libel insurance is purchased or not, all persons connected with student publications obviously should try to avoid becoming involved in libel suits. There are no substitutes for knowing the libel laws of a particular state and careful checking of copy. Certain kinds of material are worth an extra careful check. Richard Cardwell notes that most libel suits stem from contributed items, not from copy which originates with the publication itself. He believes that advertisements, wire copy, columns, news releases, and letters to the editor should be checked closely.[38] William Alfred indicates that crime news, gossip columns, April Fool editions, letters to the editor, criticisms and reviews, advertisements, and student government reports carry special libel dangers.[39]

Kenneth S. Devol has provided some useful guidelines to reduce the dangers of libel in the campus press:

Careless reporting and editing often result in libel judgments.

Coverage of controversial issues, especially those involving courts, must be handled carefully.

Stories dealing with legal issues should be based on evidence submitted for the record, not on off-the-record hearsay, rumor or statements. They should include the exact words and phrases used in the legal document, not a reporter's "augmented" version.

The newspaper must be prepared to prove the truth of the statements in question or to substantiate its right of fair comment or privilege. Repeating statements of others does not legally excuse the newspaper from answering to charges of libel.

Improper identification of persons can be disastrous. Simply deleting a name is not a dependable safeguard if the person is still identifiable—such as through his occupation or title, or if the person is likely to be confused with others.

Also disastrous can be journalistic attempts at humor, sarcasm, slang and fictionalizing.

All letters to the editor should carry signatures and should contain such further identification as ID number, major, class or address. Editors should contact writers if there is any question about the contents of the letters.

Headlines demand special care because of their attempts at brevity and impact.

Danger surrounds treatment of pictures in cropping, writing cutlines, juxtaposition and makeup.

Corrections of serious errors should be straightforward. No attempt should be made to "weasel out" of the situation, to fix blame, to be "cute" or to be argumentative.

When legal dangers are detected, editors should seek advice rather than to try to "doctor" the item or to disguise it.

If in doubt, kill it. An editor's hunch is often his best judgment.[40]

SUMMARY

Libel judgments against the student press are rare. In many states, public schools are immune from such suits under the doctrine of "sovereign immunity." Moreover, the student press usually libels its friends (other students and school administrators). In most cases the school can discipline wrongdoers without court action.

Nevertheless, libel suits have been filed as a result of student writings. Advisers and administrators are not immune from libel suits and run some risks, since anyone who was in a position to stop publication of the libelous matter and failed to do so can be sued. To protect themselves, advisers and administrators should instruct students as to the dangers of libel and carefully check copy. Contributed items (e.g., letters to the editor) and yearbook captions carry special libel dangers. Advisers and administrators should also check to see whether their schools carry libel insurance to cover employees and agents, or whether they would be "saved harmless" in such suits by their school districts or are otherwise protected by state law.

CHAPTER THREE

OBSCENITY

THE STUDENT PRESS has not escaped the problem of obscenity. With a change in sexual attitudes among American youth, students in recent years have become bolder in their means of expression. In the late 1960s a rash of four-letter words in student publications led to censorship efforts, distribution problems, editor firings, student expulsions, and other turmoil. Many of these cases are documented in this book.

Part of the ferment resulted from the rubberlike definitions of obscenity that have emerged from the courts. A variable standard has been applied which Robert C. McClure and William B. Lockhart, two leading experts in obscenity, have defined as "the obscenity of an image changing with time, place and the psychological constitution of the beholder."[1] Or, as has been described elsewhere: "Obscenity lies in the eye of the beholder."[2] Under these definitions the only material considered constitutionally obscene is material "treated" as hard-core pornography. Another writer has noted:

> Censorship of material that is not intrinsically hard-core pornography can be permitted when the manner of marketing and the primary audience to which it is marketed indicate that it is being treated as hard-core pornography—that its function in that setting is to nourish fantasies of the sexually immature. In these circumstances, both the panderer and the members of his sexually immature audience treat the material as if it were hard-core pornography.[3]

The current obscenity definitions tie in with developing court decisions involving free expression protections of the First

Amendment. Courts consistently have held that if the material in question is *not* obscene, it deserves First Amendment protection; if it *is* obscene, it is not protected. For the adviser and the student journalist, court definitional latitude tends to be restrictive. "Obscenity" in some instances has been closely related to "profanity" and "vulgarity," with decisions going against the students and the student publications involved.

FOUR-LETTER WORDS

The problem of the four-letter word, primarily the use of the earthy versions of copulate and defecate, has been centered principally in the college and university press. Since high schools usually are under more strict administrative control, in officially sanctioned publications the problem has not been a major point of concern. The words have characterized high school underground newspapers, however.

In the late 1960s the use of four-letter words in college and university publications was modish. Some editors seemed bent on pointing up societal contradictions (to their thinking) by flouting the taboos and conventions surrounding these words. By 1970, though, interest in the fad among college student editors seemed to wane. A study of the University of California's (Berkeley) student newspaper disclosed only sporadic use of language "difficult for the older generation to accept." News and editorial matter for the most part were free of such terms. "The intelligently edited publications are recognizing that an educated society can express itself with greater precision and clarity and taste than is possible with the language of the battlefield and the back alley," the report concluded.[4]

A CASE OF "OBSCENITY"

Because the definition of obscenity is so flexible, court convictions involving obscenity are relatively few. An outright conviction of a student under an obscenity statute came in March 1969. A college editor in Michigan was found guilty of "distributing a lewd, obscene, indecent, and filthy" article. The decision was affirmed in the Michigan Court of Appeals.[5]

The circumstances of the case:

James Wasserman, editor of the *Lanthorn* of Grand Valley State College, Allendale, had written a short fiction piece entitled

"A Typical Day in the Life of J. Oswald Jones." Originally it had been written to fulfill an assignment in a creative writing class where it received a grade of "A." When it appeared in the *Lanthorn,* however, Wasserman was arrested. Distributing obscene material in Michigan is a "high misdemeanor" that carries a possible penalty of one year in jail and a $1,000 fine.

Following a trial, Ottawa County Circuit Court Judge Raymond L. Smith imposed a sentence of $100 "on costs." Wasserman appealed.

In the Michigan Court of Appeals the Smith ruling was affirmed. But one judge, S. Jerome Bronson, dissented, indicating that the affirmation was a "dangerous step in the direction of thought control." He continued: "People, college students among them, ought to be protected from the over-eager use of prosecutoral machinery such as here implemented." Although he recognized that "certain words" appearing in the article may have been used primarily for their shock value, Judge Bronson did not believe the article obscene in a constitutional sense.

Likewise, Wasserman still contended his story was "definitely not obscene." He said the real reason for his conviction was not the "obscene" nature of the story but rather that prior to publication of the offending article "the Ottawa County Sheriff's Department didn't like a few things we did in the newspaper."[6]

PROFANITY AND VULGARITY

Words do not have to be construed as "obscene" in order for a student publication—particularly in high schools—to get into trouble. One case involved "profanity and vulgarity."

Two students at Earl Warren High School in Downey, California, distributed off campus copies of a newspaper named *Oink.* They were suspended from school for ten days and stripped of their student body offices (one was student body president, the other a senior class representative).

In the resulting court test, Judge Avery Crary ruled the school was within its rights to impose the penalties.[7] The school had suspended the students because *Oink* contained "profane and vulgar" expressions. Said the court:

> Neither "pornography" nor "obscenity," as defined by law, need to be established to constitute a violation of the [school] rules against profanity or vulgarity, or as a reason

for interference with discipline, or to justify the apprehension of experienced school administrators as to the impair-
ment of the school's educational process in the instant case.

One point of contention raised by the students was that the
publication had not been distributed on campus and therefore
was outside the school administration ruling against distribution
of profane and vulgar publications. This contention was slapped
down by the court: first, because the two students knew that other
students were entering the campus for class and also knew and
intended that *Oink* would be distributed on campus; and second,
because "the school authorities are responsible for the morals of
the students while going to and from school, as well as during the
time they are on campus" (see also Chapter 9).

In his opinion Judge Crary noted that the right to criticize
and to dissent is protected to high school students. "A student
may express his opinion on campus, even on controversial subjects." However, the student must do so "without materially and
substantially interfering with the requirement of appropriate discipline and without colliding with the rights of others."

THE DOWNEY GUIDELINES

In the decision's aftermath, the Downey School Board
adopted a ten-point policy statement on student newspapers, spell-
ing out rigid restrictions on school newspaper publication. The
guidelines provided that school papers:

    1. Shall be free of profanity, vulgarity and words which
have acquired undesirable meanings.
    2. Shall contain no statements derisive of any race, color,
religion, or national origin.
    3. Shall show no disrespect for law enforcement or the
institution of marriage, nor the generally accepted mores
of society.
    4. Shall not advocate illegal acts of any kind, including
the use of illegal drugs.
    5. Shall not imply approval of the use of tobacco or
liquor by high school students.
    6. Shall avoid editorial material which implies that cheat-
ing is an acceptable practice.
    7. Shall avoid naming and publicizing students who run
afoul of the law.
    8. Expressions of opinion in an article on controversial

subjects are encouraged but shall be clearly identified, by means of a by-line, as the opinion of the writer only.

9. Editors and staffs shall refrain from using the school newspaper for the promotion of personal and private interests. It is not to be used for publicizing their friends undeservedly, nor to ridicule or disparage those who are not their friends.

10. The district shall assume responsibility for funding newspapers.[8]

STUDENT EXPULSION

Another problem caused by freer use of words is student expulsion for possession of an "obscene" publication. In Belleville, Michigan, a high school student was expelled after having been found by school authorities with a copy of an underground newspaper in his possession. The principal reported that the student had violated a school directive prohibiting "offensively profane" or "disgustingly smutty" literature on school grounds.

In the resulting court case Judge Thomas P. Thornton of Detroit ruled the student's expulsion unfair.[9] The court pointed out that on the shelves of the school library could be found J. D. Salinger's *Catcher in the Rye* as well as *Harper's Magazine,* both of which contained four-letter words similar to those appearing in the *Argus,* the underground newspaper. "If *Argus* is obscene within the meaning of the school principal's directive, both *Catcher in the Rye* and *Harper's* must be obscene," the judge said.

PAPISH

A case which resulted in a restrictive ruling concerning a student expulsion occurred at the University of Missouri.[10] Barbara Susan Papish, a 32-year-old graduate student in journalism, was dismissed from the university for her part in distributing on campus a paper called *Free Press Underground.* The particular issue distributed (February 1969) contained two features which the university termed "indecent." One was a front-page cartoon depicting policemen raping the Statue of Liberty and the Goddess of Justice; the other was a headline featuring the four-letter word for copulation. Miss Papish was on disciplinary probation at the time she distributed the papers.

Following her expulsion she sought reinstatement through the federal courts, contending that she had a federally protected right to attend a state university in which she was not a resident.

The initial decision was rendered in federal district court in 1971. Miss Papish's reinstatement was denied. Chief Judge William H. Becker delivered the opinion—one closely aligned to the "variable obscenity" tenet. The opinion made much of the fact that distribution of the *Free Press Underground* took place in a "hallowed" section of the university's campus and also at a place traversed by many persons under 18 years of age. (The "hallowed" area: the Memorial Tower and related structures dedicated to the memory of students who died in the armed forces in World Wars I and II. Also in the vicinity: a nonsectarian chapel for prayer and meditation.)

The university community is comprised mainly of persons "younger and less sophisticated" than those persons in society as a whole who are interested in social comment, the judge noted. This audience was not a proper one for the "indecent obscenity" of the publication—and the publication's obscene character was recognized by the plaintiff herself.

Further, the judge proscribed high moral standards for university students. Citing *Baird* v. *State Bar of Arizona* (401 U.S. 1) and In re *Stolar* (401 U.S. 3), he implied that student moral standards were no different from the exhibition of superior moral standards that may be required to practice law.

Miss Papish appealed the decision to the Eighth U.S. Circuit Court of Appeals. That court affirmed the lower court's decision, stating that Miss Papish's university dismissal was neither "arbitrary, unreasonable nor capricious." The court expressed no view on whether the *Free Press Underground* contained legally obscene material.

Miss Papish then appealed the decision to the U.S. Supreme Court,[11] where on March 19, 1973, her reinstatement was ordered. The high court also shunned ruling on whether the underground newspaper was obscene. However, it did comment that the university had no right under these circumstances to expel a student for expressing his ideas in print form and then circulating them.

IMPOUNDING BY PRINCIPAL

In the fall of 1971 copies of a mimeographed literary magazine, *Streams of Conscience,* were seized and impounded by the principal of John Dewey High School in the Coney Island section of Brooklyn, New York. The principal, Sol Levine, contended that the magazine, edited by two Dewey students, contained a poem and an essay "which society considers obscene." The students, with the help of the New York Civil Liberties Union, contested.

Following a hearing, Federal Judge Jack B. Weinstein ordered the magazine's immediate release.[12] The words and context of the two works were not obscene and did not go beyond community standards, the judge ruled. He added that the material was "high in a literary sense and of high and considerable quality."

ADVISER DISGUST

The new freedom of expression has caused dismay in the ranks of advisers. At the college level, when the student newspaper at Wayne State University (Detroit, Mich.) was taken over by a group of self-proclaimed black revolutionaries, the faculty adviser quit in protest to the "propaganda" and "bloody vulgarity."[13] Frank P. Gill had been adviser to the Wayne State *Collegian* for 21 years. During 1968 the paper (renamed the *South End*) had become one of the nation's most politically controversial student newspapers. Its editor had proclaimed:

> I'm not a traditional campus newspaperman. There's nothing in the [old campus newspaper] that was relevant to me. We [blacks] are not interested in the "honor" of running a paper. The only validity we can give for being down here running around with college students is aiding the revolution.[14]

In announcing his resignation, Gill reported a change in acceptance of the paper by students. "It used to be that you couldn't find a copy by midafternoon, and the night students always complained. Now you fall all over the piles."[15]

PRINTER "CENSORSHIP"

Other problems have involved printer refusal to set "obscene" words in type. Print shop managers—and sometimes employees—either object to setting copy that does not measure up to their own ethical standards or are fearful of legal prosecution.

At the University of Kansas, fifty university printing service employees walked off their jobs when the chancellor guaranteed noninterference with a Black Student Union publication. The printers said setting three obscene words in the issue would make them vulnerable to obscenity charges.[16]

A printer in Merced, California, refused to handle "vulgar" language for the Merced College *Mercury,* stating: "I would not help to sow evil among the young people of the community."[17]

In Berkeley, California, the editor of the University of California humor magazine, the *Pelican,* quit after a private printing firm substituted dashes and initials for various words in the magazine. "They even changed 'god-damn' to 'G.D.,' " the editor said. In retort the printer stated that the reason for the changes was only in part a fear of legal reprisal. "We just used a few dashes. To leave the words intact wouldn't have been in good taste."[18]

KORN

Another case involving printer refusal to publish questionable material occurred at the University of Maryland.[19] There students sought to print a picture of a burning American flag on the cover of a student feature magazine, the *Argus.*

In the fall of 1969 *Argus* editors met with university representatives to arrange for a printer for the magazine. A printer was selected, but when *Argus* copy containing the offending cover arrived at his shop, the printer refused to print the cover, believing he would be subject to prosecution under Maryland law. The statute of concern: "No Person shall publicly mutilate, defile, defy, trample upon, or by word or act cast contempt upon any such flag, standard, color, ensign or shield of the United States or of the State of Maryland." The definition of "flag, standard, color, ensign or shield" included any "copy, picture or representation thereof."

A second printer was named, and he began production work. In the meantime a university official informed students that the state attorney general had affirmed the first printer's fears—publication of the cover would indeed violate the Maryland law. Armed with this opinion, the university proceeded to effectively stop publication by informing the second printer it would not pay for the work if the cover were printed. So the magazine appeared without the planned cover.

Students brought suit against various university officials, contending the Maryland statute unconstitutional. The case went to a federal court, where a decision was rendered. In its decision the court applied the ruling of *Street* v. *New York* (394 U.S. 576, 1969). In that case the U.S. Supreme Court reversed a criminal conviction under a New York law couched in almost identical language as that of Maryland. The defendant in the New York case had burned an American flag on a New York City street corner. As the flag burned the defendant made statements concerning his act. In the *Street* decision the Supreme Court did not consider whether or not the New York law was unconstitutional on its face. Instead, it held that it was unconstitutionally applied because it permitted the defendant to be punished for merely speaking defiant or contemptuous words about the flag.

In applying *Street* to *Korn,* the district court said that the proposed *Argus* cover picture was only expression in the form of art, and *Street* clearly required the protection of such expression. In view of the absence of any evidence showing that suppression of *Argus* contents was necessary to preserve order and discipline on campus, the court held that the Maryland statute was unconstitutionally applied. As in *Street,* it did not reach the question of the statute's constitutionality.

POST OFFICE CONTROLS

The basic federal antiobscenity statute has been used by federal authorities in efforts to control mailing of obscene material. The law (18 U.S.C., Sec. 1461) declares that obscene materials are "nonmailable matter and shall not be conveyed in the mails or delivered from any post office or by any letter carrier." Those found guilty of mailing obscene matter are subject to a $5,000 fine or five-year imprisonment or both for the first offense.

In one landmark case a conviction under the law was returned and upheld by the U.S. Supreme Court.[20] Other indictments under the law have resulted in dismissals. The principal difficulty is one of definition: What is obscenity? In its first effort to define it the Supreme Court said that obscene material "deals with sex in a manner appealing to prurient interest" as well as being "utterly without redeeming social importance" and against "contemporary community standards" (*Roth* v. *U.S.,* 354 U.S. 476). Subsequent cases pointed up the difficulty of applying this standard, and in June 1973 the Court agreed on new guidelines in an effort to isolate hard-core pornography from expression protected by the First Amendment.[21]

Illustrative of the problem of definition in postal application was a New Orleans case where an underground newspaper was charged with mailing obscene material. The biweekly had run a photograph of a nude man masturbating in front of a wall covered with nude female pinups. A federal court dismissed the indictment. The court noted that a portion of a publication can taint the whole only by rendering it "salacious in its entirety." Most of the 16-page newspaper was devoted to "libidinally neutral" news reports, poetry, artwork, and discussion of topics generally of interest to the particular community the newspaper sought to serve.

The court said the picture itself was not obscene, although it was "shocking and repellent" and "patently offensive to any general audience." The dominant theme of the work did not appeal to prurient interests and arouse lustful thoughts but "ridiculed other publications [e.g. *Playboy*] that do attempt such an appeal."[22]

Partly because of the problem of definition, the post office recently has been concentrating on dealers who mail questionable material to persons who file a complaint. Under authority of a 1970 law, a family receiving a pandering advertisement which it finds offensive has authority to ask that its members receive no more mail of any kind from the sender.[23]

SAFE GUIDELINES

Decisions indicate that often a college publication will not get itself into legal trouble simply by being "obscene." In *Antonelli* v. *Hammond*,[24] a federal court ruled that publication of alleged obscenity in a college newspaper was not of sufficient significance to upset the school environment. "Obscenity in a campus newspaper is not the type of occurrence apt to be significantly disruptive of an orderly and disciplined educational process," said the court (see also Chapter 1). In high schools, though, if material can be construed as obscene (or even profane and/or vulgar) and if it tends to disrupt the educational process, a decision may go against the publication and the personnel involved.

For high schools especially, the admonition, as indicated by court decisions, is a restrictive one. If personnel involved with procuring and distributing student publications want to protect their rights of free expression, no words or phrases that can be construed as being obscene should be printed.

SUMMARY

The U.S. Supreme Court in the late 1960s established guide-lines to enable courts and juries to define obscene material. These proved legally unworkable, and courts turned to examining modes of distribution to bring convictions in obscenity cases. Was the material advertised in a pandering manner? Was it displayed in such a way as to constitute a blatant assault on the privacy of those who did not want to see it? Was it likely to fall into the hands of children? Now, as this book goes to press, it appears that the Court, arming itself with a new set of guidelines, may be re-turning to a definitional concentration.

In cases involving high schools, courts have tended to view obscenity cases narrowly, from both a definitional and a distribu-tive standpoint. Trouble will likely result even if "profanity" or "vulgarity" is published. A high school administration, because its jurisdiction involves pupils in the 14–18 age group, may re-ceive court and patron support if it clamps down with restrictive measures.

In any case, student editors have found that they cannot de-viate too far from the acceptable standards of their community and firms with which they must do business. If they do, their publishing efforts may be short-lived.

CHAPTER FOUR

CONTEMPT

IN 1966 A GRAND JURY in Lane County, Oregon, was investigating drug use on the University of Oregon campus. Annette Buchanan, an editor of the Oregon *Daily Emerald,* was subpoenaed as a witnesss and refused to tell the grand jury the names of seven unidentified drug users she had quoted in a news story. As a result she was fined $300 for contempt of court.

Numerous professional journalism organizations sprang to her defense. They maintained, as did Miss Buchanan, that forced disclosures of confidential news sources are unethical and also violate First Amendment press freedom guarantees. But the Oregon Supreme Court upheld her conviction.[1]

Miss Buchanan was guilty of contempt when she disobeyed an order of a court. Congress, state legislatures, and even some semijudicial administrative bodies have the power to punish those who interfere with the conduct of investigative matters. But most contempt citations are issued by courts for interference with the administration of justice.

Contempt may be either direct or indirect. Direct contempt can result from failure to obey an order of a court (as in the case of Miss Buchanan) or any other activity within the confines of the court that would seriously interfere with a judicial proceeding. Creating a disturbance in a courtroom or taking photographs during a trial could result in a citation. Indirect (also called "constructive") contempt is activity away from the courtroom that is threatening to the judicial process. A grossly false or inaccurate report of a trial, for example, might be indirectly contemptuous of the court. Citations for indirect contempt are rare, however; in both categories of contempt, a clear and present danger to the administration of justice must exist.

SHIELD LAWS

In some states newsmen cannot be ordered by a state court
to reveal their news sources. Alabama, Alaska, Arizona, Arkansas,
California, Illinois, Indiana, Kentucky, Louisiana, Maryland,
Michigan, Montana, Nevada, New Jersey, New Mexico, New
York, Ohio, Pennsylvania, and Rhode Island have "shield" laws
that protect newsmen from being forced by a state court or legislature to disclose sources of news. In at least thirteen of these
states, student journalists seem to be protected along with professional reporters and editors.

Somewhat typical is the shield law of California, which reads
in part:

> A publisher, editor, reporter, or other person con-
> nected with or employed upon a newspaper, or by a press
> association or wire service, cannot be adjudged in con-
> tempt by a court, the Legislature, or any administrative
> body for refusing to disclose the source of any information
> procured for publication and published in a newspaper.[2]

If shield laws clearly defined such words as reporter and
newspaper, student journalists might be disqualified, since it
is doubtful that state legislatures intended to give them this privilege. However, most shield laws were passed before student reporters became so rambunctious, and the wording of many shield
laws is so broad that almost anyone who has anything to do with
a publication (including an adviser or administrator) might be
protected.

States that do not have shield laws have pointed to this
problem of definition as a reason for questioning the wisdom of
such statutes. In the *Buchanan* case, the Oregon Supreme Court
said:

> Assuming that legislators are free to experiment with
> such definitions, it would be dangerous business for courts
> . . . to extend to an employee of a "respectable" news-
> paper a privilege which would be denied to an employee
> of a disreputable newspaper; or an episodic pamphleteer;
> or to a free-lance writer seeking to sell a story on the open
> market; or, indeed to a shaggy non-conformist who wishes
> only to write out his message and nail it to a tree.

But few legislators have tried to experiment with such definitions. Only Illinois, Indiana, Louisiana, New Mexico, New

York, Pennsylvania, and Rhode Island have defined "newspaper" in a shield law sense. In Louisiana, New Mexico, and Rhode Island a newspaper "must be issued at regular intervals and [have] a paid circulation."[3] This would seem to include many student newspapers. However, Illinois specifies that a newspaper must have a "paid general circulation."[4] Indiana requires that to claim the privilege a journalist must be connected with "a weekly, semiweekly, triweekly or daily newspaper that conforms to postal regulations, [which has] been published for five consecutive years in the same city or town and which has a paid circulation of two per cent of the population of the county in which it is published."[5]

Pennsylvania protects reporters for newspapers which come out at least once a week and are "intended for general distribution and circulation."[6] New York requires that a reporter or editor must work for a newspaper that appears at least once a week and has a second-class postage permit.[7]

Only Alaska, Illinois, Indiana, New Mexico, and New York attempt to define "reporter" or "journalist." In Alaska, Illinois, and New Mexico, shield protection is limited to "a person regularly engaged in the business of writing and collecting news for publication."[8] The word "business," if interpreted narrowly, might exclude at least some student journalists. In Indiana a journalist must receive "his or her principal income from legitimate gathering, writing, editing and interpretation of the news."[9] The New York law protects only "professional" journalists engaged in news gathering "for gain or livelihood,"[10] which also seems to exclude student reporters.

High school journalists appear to be clearly excluded from shield protection in New York and Indiana and probably excluded in Alaska, Illinois, New Mexico, and Pennsylvania. Only in Indiana and New York are the laws worded so that most reporters for college publications might not be eligible.

Shield laws are far from complete protection for any journalist, however. They usually are interpreted to cover only the sources of published news—not documents or notes, sources of unpublished information, or cases where the newsman witnesses a crime. In the shield law states of Alaska, Arkansas, Illinois, Louisiana, and New Mexico, no newsman may protect his sources if the public interest requires their disclosure.[11]

WHAT IS A NEWSPAPER?

Despite the broad wording of most shield laws, students who try to claim the privilege could run into difficulties. For example, it could be argued that a student newspaper is not a newspaper in a legal sense. In *Zucker* v. *Panitz*,[12] which concerned an attempt by students to run a paid editorial advertisement in the New Rochelle (N.Y.) High School *Huguenot Herald,* a high school principal maintained that the school newspaper was not a newspaper in the usual meaning of the word but instead was a "beneficial educational device." A U.S. District Court found that the *Huguenot Herald* was a "forum for the dissemination of ideas" within the context of an educational environment and "more than a mere activity time and place sheet," but stopped short of a clearer ruling on this aspect of the case.

Lee v. *Board of Regents*,[13] which dealt with the right of students to run paid editorial advertisements in the *Royal Purple* of Wisconsin State University, Whitewater, shows that this argument might not work too well for a college publication. In this case a U.S. District Court judge said that a campus newspaper meets the general definition of a newspaper as "a paper printed and distributed, at stated intervals . . . to convey news, advocate opinions, etc., now usually containing also advertisements and other matters of public interest."

Is an underground newspaper a "newspaper"? In *State* v. *Knops*,[14] the underground Madison (Wis.) *Kaleidoscope* was declared by a Wisconsin court in a contempt proceeding to be a newspaper, and its editor was considered to be a journalist. However, the editor was 27 years old, and the newspaper was circulated among college students. A court might take a different view of an underground newspaper produced by and circulated among high school students.

CONFIDENTIAL ASSOCIATIONS;
INANIMATE MATERIALS

The professional journalist has some legal protection for his confidential associations, tape recordings, notes, and photographs. In a 1970 case involving *New York Times* reporter Earl Caldwell and his relationship with the Black Panthers (434 F. 2d 1081), a U.S. Court of Appeals indicated that a grand jury could require inanimate materials or testimony regarding confidential associations only when there is "compelling or overriding" need for them. In *Knops* the Wisconsin Supreme Court subsequently ruled that an underground newspaper editor who refused to testify about a letter he received from a group claiming "credit" for the bombing of a University of Wisconsin building was in contempt because he had knowledge of a specific crime. "The need for answers is overriding . . . to say the least," said the court. (Knops was sentenced to six months in jail.) However, the *Caldwell* case did set some limits on "fishing" through a professional reporter's notes and tapes for unspecified information; a student reporter might be accorded similar protection.[15]

INJUNCTIONS

Occasionally injunctions (to prevent a person or group from carrying out a given action) have been used to restrain the student press. A district attorney obtained an injunction prohibiting the distribution of a literary magazine at Cornell University because he believed an article in the magazine was obscene.[16] Publication of the Grand Valley State College (Mich.) student newspaper was enjoined for 20 days after the newspaper published an allegedly obscene article.[17] If a court's injunction is not obeyed, a violator may be held in contempt.

On at least one occasion a student newspaper sought an injunction to protect its rights. In 1971 the Stanford *Daily* asked a U.S. District Court to enjoin a reoccurrence of a police search of its offices. The *Daily* maintained that the search violated First, Fifth, and Fourteenth Amendment press freedom guarantees.

The search followed a demonstration and sit-in at Stanford University Hospital which ended in a violent confrontation between demonstrators and Palo Alto police. More than 20 people were injured, including 13 policemen; damage to university property was estimated at $100,000.

Three days after the demonstration the police, armed with a search warrant, spent 45 minutes in *Daily* offices looking for photographs taken during the sit-in and going through wastebaskets, desks, and stacks of old newspapers seeking materials that might help them identify participants. The search failed to turn up anything useful.

Sigma Delta Chi, professional society of journalists, called the action by police a "violation of propriety and privacy" and "not one bit less loathsome for having been perpetrated against a campus newspaper rather than an established independent publication."[18] Felicity Barringer, 20-year-old editor of the *Daily*, declared that unpublished information such as notes, tape recordings, or photographs should be "ours to keep confidential." To open such unpublished materials to outside agencies "would break down the relationship of trust between newsmakers and news gatherers that is vital to accurate and complete reportage," she argued.[19]

In 1972 a U.S. District Court declared illegal the police search of *Daily* offices. Judge Robert F. Peckham noted that searches of a newspaper office

> are impermissible in all but a very few situations. A search warrant should be permitted only in the rare circumstances where there is a clear showing that important materials will be destroyed or removed from the jurisdiction and a restraining order would be futile.

Peckham declined to issue an injunction against further searches, saying he had no reason to believe police would conduct another search of *Daily* offices.[20] The Santa Clara, California, district attorney's office planned to appeal Peckham's declaratory judgment.[21]

SUMMARY

Contempt of court is not likely to be a problem for the student journalist unless he is covering trials or reporting possible criminal activity. Some danger exists in stories on drug use. In many states a court may order a student reporter to reveal his confidential news sources and hold him in contempt if he refuses. Even in states with shield laws, some doubt exists as to whether a reporter for a high school or underground publication is able to claim this privilege. In most shield law states, college reporters probably are protected.

If the educational process is seriously threatened or if laws are being broken, a high school or college may obtain an injunction to restrain the student press. If a court's injunction is not obeyed, a violator may be held in contempt.

CHAPTER FIVE

ADVERTISING

AMERICAN COURTS HAVE RULED consistently that privately owned publications may accept or reject advertising as their judgment best dictates. Most publishers are considered to be involved in ordinary private businesses. Although they perform important public services, they do not have to accept all advertisements submitted to them. "If a newspaper were required to accept an advertisement, it could be compelled to publish a news item," one court reasoned (*Shuck* v. *Carroll Daily Herald,* 215 Iowa 1276).

Publicly financed student publications have also rejected advertisements on almost any grounds they wished to use, and their policies usually have not been challenged in court. Because of public relations concerns and the *in loco parentis* idea, high school and college publications have rejected advertising that many commercial publishers would accept. The most commonly prohibited advertisements found by Kenneth S. Devol in his 1965 study of 65 college newspapers were those that:

had hints of racial bias
were in "poor taste"
offered matrimony
dealt with areas requiring professional knowledge, such as medicine
violated local, state, or federal laws
offered the services of spiritualists or fortune tellers
did not contain the name of the product or the name of the advertiser
were identified only by a postal box number
were suspected of being fraudulent
were submitted by those whose accounts were in arrears
offered the sale of alcoholic beverages
could detract from the good name of the school.[1]

Publicly financed student publications still seem safe in rejecting any advertising of a purely commercial nature. But recent court rulings indicate that "editorial" advertisements may *not* be rejected by a publicly owned or publicly controlled facility if such rejection violates constitutional free speech guarantees.

ADVERTISING AS FREE SPEECH

In *Times* v. *Sullivan* (376 U.S. 254) the U.S. Supreme Court in 1964 called advertising "an important outlet for the promulgation of information and ideas by persons who do not themselves have access to publishing facilities." The high court differentiated ordinary commercial advertisements from "editorial" advertisements and indicated that the latter deserve constitutional free speech protection when they involve "matters of the highest public concern."

Advertising as a matter of free speech was carried a step further in 1967 when the California Supreme Court ruled (434 P. 2d 982) that political advertising within the protection of the First Amendment could not be refused by a publicly owned transit authority "for reasons of administrative convenience" if the transit authority "open[s] a forum for the expression of ideas" by allowing advertising on its buses. The advertisements in question, sponsored by a group seeking an end to the Vietnam war, dealt with "opinions and beliefs within the ambit of First Amendment protection," declared the court.

ZUCKER

In 1969 *Zucker* v. *Panitz*[2] opened the door for high school students who want to run "editorial" advertising in student newspapers. A group of students at a New Rochelle (N.Y.) High School formed an Ad Hoc Student Committee Against the War in Vietnam and tried to run a paid advertisement in their student newspaper, the *Huguenot Herald*. The advertisement read:

> The United States government is pursuing a policy in Viet Nam which is both repugnant to moral and international law and dangerous to the future of humanity. We can stop it. We must stop it.

The editorial board of the newspaper approved the advertisement, but Dr. Adolph Panitz, principal of the school, refused to allow its publication. Laura Zucker, student chairman of the editorial board, and other students brought suit, alleging that the purpose of the student newspaper was "to provide a forum for the dissemination of ideas and information" within the school and that prohibition of the advertisement constituted an abridgement of constitutional rights of free speech.

Defendant Panitz argued that because citizens have no right of access to a privately owned newspaper, students have no right of access to a school-sponsored newspaper. Panitz also argued that the school had a long-standing policy of limiting advertisements and news articles to matters directly related to school activities, and that only purely commercial advertising was accepted by the *Huguenot Herald*.

A U.S. District Court found for the plaintiffs, however. Judge Charles M. Metzer ruled that the rejection of the advertisement was a violation of free expression rights. Different policy considerations govern whether a privately owned newspaper has a duty to grant access to its pages, said Metzer, because state involvement can be demonstrated in a public school newspaper. Metzer noted that past issues of the *Huguenot Herald* contained articles, editorials, and letters to the editor on controversial topics:

> The presence of articles concerning the draft and student opinion of United States participation in the war shows that the war is considered to be a school-related subject. This being the case, there is no logical reason to permit news stories on the subject and preclude student advertising.

Since the *Huguenot Herald* was open to free expression of ideas in news and editorial columns and letters to the editor, "[i]t is patently unfair in light of the free speech doctrine to close to the students the forum which they deem effective to present their views," Metzer ruled. He ordered New Rochelle school officials not to interfere with student rights of free expression in the *Huguenot Herald*.

LEE

A similar case in 1969 on the college level, *Lee* v. *Board of Regents*,[3] upheld the right of students to run paid "editorial" advertisements in the *Royal Purple* of Wisconsin State University (Whitewater). The plaintiffs submitted to the *Royal Purple* advertisements which (1) described the purposes of a university employees' union and announced a meeting on safety regulations, (2) condemned discrimination on the basis of color or creed, and (3) opposed the Vietnam war. All were rejected. The *Royal Purple* would not accept advertising on "political issues" and limited meeting advertising to "come to the meeting" messages. Lee and others then asked for a declaratory judgment that their constitutional rights of freedom of expression had been violated by the university.

U.S. District Court Judge James E. Doyle, citing *Zucker,* ruled that the *Royal Purple*'s rejection of these editorial advertisements was "an impermissible form of censorship" and "a denial of free speech and expression in violation of the First and Fourteenth Amendments." As a campus newspaper, the *Royal Purple* "constitutes an important forum for the dissemination of news and expression of opinion. As such a forum, it should be open to anyone who is willing to pay to have his views published therein—not just to commercial advertisers."

Doyle dismissed the university's arguments that the students could have their views published in letters-to-the-editor columns by pointing out:

> It is readily apparent that a paid advertisement can be cast in such a form as to command much greater attention than a letter to the editor. Large type, photographs, repeated publication, and full pages of space are some of the modes of expression available in an editorial advertisement that might not be available in a letter to the editor.

In 1971 a U.S. Court of Appeals affirmed the district court's ruling. The appeals court said that "a state public body which disseminates paid advertising of a commercial type may not reject other paid advertising on the basis that it is editorial in character." The court called the *Royal Purple* a "state facility" but added: "The case does not pose the question whether defendants could have excluded all advertising nor whether there are other conceivable limitations on advertising which could be properly imposed."

Wisconsin State had argued that the *Royal Purple*'s advertising policy was a "reasonable means of protecting the university from embarrassment and the staff from the difficulty of exercising judgment as to material which may be obscene, libelous, or subversive." The appeals court cited *Tinker* which said, in part, that "undifferentiated fear or apprehension of disturbance is not enough to overcome the right of freedom of expression."

IMPLICATIONS

The implications of the *Zucker* and *Lee* decisions have bothered many advisers, administrators, and staff members of student publications. Mary Mills, adviser to the *Royal Purple*, wrote prior to the Wisconsin State decision:

> If the paper loses its right to reject ads, it will be at the mercy of anyone who wishes to buy space regardless of the quality of his product or the suitability of it for advertising in our paper. The paper would also be required—I believe—to accept advertising regardless of the availability of space in a particular issue. And I wonder if we must accept any article anyone wishes to submit in the name of guaranteeing his right to free speech?[4]

The decisions, however, covered only paid "editorial" advertisements submitted by students to public school-sponsored newspapers. Furthermore, *Zucker* seemed to turn on the fact that the *Huguenot Herald* had run articles on the Vietnam war. Could a high school newspaper be forced to accept an advertisement on a subject it had not discussed in its news columns? Could it be forced to accept an advertisement if it did not run any advertisements? *Zucker* leaves these questions unanswered.

Lee indicates that college newspaper columns "should be open to anyone who is willing to pay to have his views published therein." But the case did not involve whether a college publication might either exclude all advertising or adopt reasonable limitations on advertising it prints. Interfering with constitutionally protected free speech is certainly not considered to be a reasonable limitation, but advertising that is commercial in nature has not been given constitutional protection.

CONTROVERSIAL ADVERTISING

Sometimes it is difficult to identify advertising that may be constitutionally protected, and schools decide not to force the issue, even though such ads are controversial. In October 1970 the Florida State *Flambeau* refused to accept an advertisement announcing a Gay Liberation Front meeting, but the newspaper was overruled by the university's Board of Publications. The

Flambeau argued that running similar advertising in the spring of 1970 had resulted in a loss of linage from local merchants. The publications board, however, agreed with the Gay Liberation Front's contention that the group had been denied "freedom of speech by a body that receives its funds from the Student Body."[5]

ILLEGAL ADVERTISING

Student journalists should be aware of federal, state, and local laws that could prohibit the publication of certain advertisements. For example, it is against federal and most state laws to publicize lotteries (see Chapter 10). Most states have statutes prohibiting fraudulent and misleading advertising.

College newspapers in Minnesota, Massachusetts, Nebraska, Ohio, Connecticut, Florida, and Virginia came under fire during academic year 1970–71 for running abortion referral advertising believed contrary to state laws.[6] The following year Ronald Sachs, editor of the University of Florida *Alligator,* decided to test the constitutionality of a Florida law which read, in part:

> Whoever knowingly advertises, prints, publishes, distributes or circulates . . . any advice, direction, information or knowledge . . . for the purpose of causing or procuring the miscarriage of any woman pregnant with child, shall be punished by imprisonment in the state prison not exceeding one year, or by fine not exceeding one thousand dollars.[7]

Sachs inserted a mimeographed list of abortion referral agencies into an issue of the *Alligator* and was arrested. His attorneys argued that the law was unconstitutionally vague and violated press freedom guarantees. County Judge Benjamin M. Trench agreed and dismissed the charges.[8]

POLICY STATEMENTS

Student publications might consider running policy statements on advertising. While unreasonable rules must be avoided, policy statements are in line with the current emphasis (discussed in Chapter 1) on letting students know what the rules are in the first place. The Ohio State *Lantern,* for example, has run the following statement in its masthead:

> The Lantern cannot accept advertising that advocates sedition or other illegal actions, violates normal standards of morality and taste or attacks an individual, race, nationality, ethnic group or religion.
>
> In case of doubt, the proffered copy, illustrations and layout will be submitted by the business manager of the Lantern to the School of Journalism Publication Committee and judged by a majority vote of members. Decisions of this committee are final. The Lantern reserves the right to refuse any advertising.
>
> The Ohio State Lantern does not restrict advertisers beyond the limits of responsible journalism and the rules imposed by the Ohio State University on all student publications.

A policy statement might also include information on space limitations and deadlines for submission of copy. Any reasonable rules which apply to all advertisers should be legally defensible.

ARTICLES

A student publication may reject an article on the basis of "editorial judgment," according to a U.S. Court of Appeals decision in *Avins* v. *Rutgers.*[9]

After the Rutgers (State University of New Jersey) *Law Review* turned down an article on constitutional law, the writer of the article tried to force the student-edited publication to accept it, claiming that his constitutional right of free speech had been abridged. But the court ruled that the *Law Review* did not have to accept every article submitted to it. "There must necessarily be a broad area of discretion," said the judge. He agreed with a lower court's decision that:

> the Editorial Board must be selective in what it publishes, and a selective process requires the exercise of opinion as to what particular subject matter will at a given time be of educational value, not only to the student body but also to subscribers.

This necessity for editorial judgment, the court continued, *"is in no wise lessened by the fact that the law review is supported, at least in part by the state"* (emphasis added).

SUMMARY

A student publication apparently may safely either exclude all advertising or adopt reasonable limitations on what advertising it prints.

Publicly financed student publications still seem safe in rejecting any advertising of a purely commercial nature. However, paid "editorial" advertisements, submitted by students and involving "matters of the highest public concern," may not be rejected "for reasons of convenience" if such rejection violates constitutional free speech guarantees. If doubt exists as to whether an advertisement falls within "the ambit of First Amendment protection" or whether an advertisement is illegal, student due process rights should be upheld. That is, there should be a right of appeal to a student-faculty committee or to a higher administrative authority.

A student publication may reject an article on the basis of "editorial judgment."

CHAPTER SIX

COPYRIGHT

To the student editor, the publications adviser, or the administrator, two aspects of copyright law are important. The first is the wisdom of copyrighting student publications; the second concerns the right to *use* copyrighted material.

There is little concern in either the commercial press or the student press about copyrighting news material. Facts and ideas themselves cannot be copyrighted, only their concrete expression. The protection extends only to the exact wording a writer uses. Also, in news coverage situations, because two reporters writing about the same facts will often use similar words, infringement is difficult to prove.

The circumstance is different, though, with fictionalized matter. Most concern about copyright is among those whose goal is to entertain rather than to report. With the voracious appetite of television, the supply of good fiction material never seems to meet the demand. The entertainment industry frets about copyright infringements. Play scripts, songs, and jokes are in short supply, and industry professionals carefully protect their rights. Since this type of matter is often used in a campus literary publication, its protection and use deserve the attention of the student publication staff and/or adviser.

Another potential area of concern to the publication staff both as to rights of protection and rights to copy includes photographs or other prints and illustrations, a primary ingredient of yearbooks. Such artwork also is subject to copyright laws.[1]

COPYRIGHT PROCEDURE

The question concerning procurement of a copyright is often raised by yearbook staffs. The answer probably depends on the publication's quality. If the annual contains several good photographs of campus scenes which the staff and/or the administration thinks might be worthy of further reproduction, the yearbook should be copyrighted.[2] The school will then have control over future use of the material. For example, a commercial newspaper might want to reproduce a picture of a campus scene; if the material has been copyrighted, the school could give permission and request a credit line. Thus the school would get a small amount of additional publicity out of the reproduction, if nothing else.

The cost of securing a copyright is minimal. More bothersome is the secretarial work and the subsequent checking. Exacting procedures must be followed in order to validate the copyright protection: (1) A copyright notice must be printed in a specific location in the printed work. (2) Two copies of the work must be sent to the Register of Copyrights. (3) The forms must be filled out. (4) The $6 fee must be paid. If one of these requirements is omitted, the copyright protection is voided.

Of particular importance is the requirement that copies bear the copyright notice in the prescribed form and in the correct position. The form: the word "Copyright" or the abbreviation "Copr." or the symbol ©, followed by the name of the copyright owner and the year of publication. The three elements of notice must appear together. Example: © Brouhaha College, 1973.

In addition the notice must appear on the title page or the page immediately following. "Page immediately following" usually means the reverse side of the title page since, when a publication is printed on both sides of pages, a "page" is regarded as one side of a leaf.

Under the present law the first term of statutory copyright runs for 28 years and may be renewed for another 28 years upon application to the copyright office at the expiration of the first term.

FAIR USE

Fair use is a use of copyrighted material even though no expressed authorization is granted by the copyright owner. Fred S. Siebert says that "fair use is a legal doctrine not to be found in the Copyright Act, but adopted by the courts in order to alleviate the limited monopoly which copyright protection gives the owner."[3]

There is no legal basis for establishing specific rules or

guidelines indicating how much use of a copyrighted work is fair use, but Siebert identifies five areas:

1. Incidental Use. A reasonable amount of material can be used incidentally or as background for new work. One of the tests applied is whether or not the use made of the copyrighted work tends to lessen the commercial sale of the original work.

2. Review and Criticism. Excerpts and quotations may be used in serious criticism. Critics may quote extensively for purposes of illustration and comment.

3. Parody and Burlesque. Although a competitive revision of a copyrighted work may be an infringement, mimicry in good faith (no matter how devastating) is considered fair use. The line between fair use and infringement is difficult to draw, and courts may rule in favor of either side in similar cases.

4. Scholarly Works and Compilations. An earlier work may be used collaterally (in addition to portions of other earlier works) but not substantially copied.

5. Use for Non-Profit Purpose. No clear-cut cases have decided that a use for an educational not-for-profit purpose is within the doctrine of fair use, but, on the other hand, it is justifiable to say that fair use is wider in situations where the commercial element is absent.[4]

ACQUIRING PERMISSION

If a considerable amount of material is to be copied from another publication for use in a student publication, written permission should be secured from the copyright holder and proper credit given. Permission usually involves an exchange of letters; a letter is prepared requesting written permission to use the material in question. The usual form for giving credit after permission is granted: "Copyright Alice Zink, 1965. Reprinted by permission."

Copyright holders are under no obligation to respond or to grant permission. Also, they may charge any amount they desire to permit utilization of the material.

USE OF COPYRIGHTED MATERIAL BY SCHOOLS

Few cases involving infringement of copyrights by schools have reached the courts. R. R. Hamilton, editor of *National School Law Reporter*, thinks this is surprising in view of the millions of dollars worth of copyrighted material used by schools each year.[5] He cites one case which, although it didn't involve student publications, illustrates the type of suit that could involve an adviser and/or a school if copyrights are overlooked.

The case concerned a suit by a copyright holder against a choral instructor and others in the Clarinda (Iowa) School District.[6] The instructor had found 25 copies of a song in the files but needed 48 more, so he used the school's duplicating machine to run them off.

A U.S. District Court found that the instructor's duplication of the material was fair and not a copyright infringement, but a U.S. Court of Appeals found for the plaintiff. The court said the fact that the defendant did not intend to infringe was immaterial; although he used the material for an educational purpose, he deprived the author of possible sales.

COPYRIGHT BY STUDENTS

Another type of problem where there is little record involves student desire to copyright his own work as it appears in a student publication. Presumably, if the student wishes to take the initiative to secure a copyright, most schools would be willing to cooperate even though the work was done under faculty supervision. Of course the student's copyright must not conflict with any copyright the school itself might secure. The school may copyright the entire contents of a yearbook, magazine, or newspaper.

If the student wants his work to be copyrighted in his own name and not that of the school, or if his work is to appear in an uncopyrighted student publication, he should get the school's permission to have a copyright line placed under his contribution's title or at the bottom of the first page on which it appears (for example: Copyright Alfred Zink, 1973). Immediately after publication he should file an application for registration with the Copyright Office, Library of Congress, Washington, D.C. 20540 (ask for form BB), pay the fee, and send *one* complete copy of the publication to the Copyright Office (not just the page or pages on which his contribution appears).[7] Material published and not copyrighted falls into the "public domain" and the author loses his rights in it.

Some universities regulate results of research done by a student under faculty supervision and making use of university facilities.[8] In such cases the student might not be able to secure a copyright. In high schools usually there is no similar problem.

SUMMARY

Most school concern with copyright involves use of copyrighted material rather than acquiring protection. Under the "fair use" doctrine, a limited amount of material may be copied without the permission of the copyright holder. If a substantial amount of the original material is to be copied exactly, permission to reproduce should be obtained. Permission usually involves only a simple exchange of letters.

CHAPTER SEVEN

ACCESS TO INFORMATION

ONE LEGAL QUESTION occasionally confronting the student newspaper's editorial staff is that of access to public meetings and records. It is an issue concerning not only the student press but also commercial newspapers. Since World War II editors, publishers, and news organizations have pressed for greater access to governmental chronicles and deliberations. Partially through the work of "freedom of information" committees of journalistic societies and organizations, most states, municipalities, and public bodies have enacted laws or handed down directives declaring the principle of open meetings and records. Forty-one states now have open records laws; thirty-eight have open meetings laws.[1]

The laws and directives vary—some are more "open" than others. In no law is it acknowledged that *every* official document and *every* public meeting should be open to public (and press) scrutiny. Some records, particularly those tending to invade personal privacy, remain secret. In addition, rules and regulations incorporated into the laws tend to throw roadblocks in the way of the public and press when they try to gain ready access to the documents or deliberations. For the student journalist there is an additional problem: Does he have "standing," equivalent to the commercial press, to see and report governmental information?

The rationale behind the principle of open records and open meetings is rooted in democratic theory of government: self-governing people need to know about the activities of their public officials in order to make fitting selections on election days. But a dilemma arises between officials and the press representing the public's "right to know." Officials sometimes seek to perpetuate their office by shielding themselves from accountability; the democratic public is sometimes fearful of unchecked power and corruption which nurse on seclusion.

RECORDS

States having open records laws differ widely both as to definition of records and degree of access permitted. Louisiana throws open "all" records, but in Massachusetts many records "public" on their face are open only when an interested person has reason to believe the public custodian may not be conducting his office properly. Laws are generally stricter in New England states where records are more jealously guarded; freer access is granted in western states.[2] The gray area in definition is: Where does a public record end and an office memorandum begin? Some states publish extensive and detailed lists of records prohibited from public view; others use only brief and general terms.[3]

The statutes usually indicate rights and restrictions associated with inspection. Some concern record safety: the records may not be removed from the office and are to be used only during office hours. Others concern office efficiency: the inspection must not unduly upset office routine. Other rules say that the purpose of the person seeking access must be "legitimate and proper."[4] This is a part of common law. In some states it has been held that "idle curiosity" on the part of the applicant is definitely not a sufficient purpose.[5] Yet in other states the motive is said not to matter.[6]

The press has the right to make copies of records. The established legal precedent is that the inspection right is practically valueless unless copying rights also are accorded.

The aspect of "standing" to see public records is of concern to the student press. Court rulings over the years give commercial press representatives such status. The rulings accept the newspaper's news-gathering function as a special interest. Inherent also is the commercial aspect: the fiscal viability of the newspaper depends on its ability to print news, including news of public affairs. For the student press the precedents here are not as strong and there are no legal rulings specifically giving the student reporter equivalent status. Also, for most student papers the commercial need to publish news is nonessential.

MEETINGS

As it concerns the commercial press, the reporter's right to attend and report public meetings is accepted under common law; the right is even clearer in the 41 states where "open meetings" statutes have been enacted. But again the problem of definition arises. Is the meeting of an executive board a public meeting? A special school board committee investigating school discipline? A meeting of a Black Student Union (BSU) at a university? Often the only way to judge is that a public meeting where rights of access accrue will be conducted with a certain formality, a characteristic not present at lower eschelon gatherings. In the case of the BSU, this was judged a private meeting by a student newspaper board of directors (the editor and a reporter were suspended on grounds that means used to obtain a story were "unethical"). But the BSU meeting was considered a public meeting by the university's chapter of Sigma Delta Chi (it condemned the suspensions).[7]

Even in states where the laws concerning definitions and access to meetings are relatively specific, there are points of contention. One controversy concerns the "executive" or closed session where a council or board shuts out the public (and reporters) ostensibly to discuss an internal matter. Newspapermen object to this procedure because no controls exist over what can be discussed. Sometimes a council, a county commission, or a school board threshes out its business in "executive" session and then convenes a public session to merely announce its decisions. The public never knows the nuances of discussion points—nuances that may be vital to the public interest.

Another point of contention concerns meetings of subcommittees of a council or a board. These frequently are closed to the public, because subcommittee members feel they need to conduct uninhibited discussion, outside public view, where wild "brainstorm" ideas can be expressed. The more open these discussions can be, the more robust and invigorated the end result, the argument states. Even the Sigma Delta Chi Committee on Advancement of Freedom of Information recognizes the right of governmental bodies on occasion to have executive sessions.[8] The public interest is not served by opening *all* deliberations of public bodies to the public and press.

OPENING RECORDS BY COURT ACTION

Especially in states where open records statutes exist, a person having standing to look at the records can usually get a court order to force the official involved to open his records. This is done, of course, in the absence of cooperation of the official. The procedure is to petition a judge to issue a writ of mandamus requiring the official to perform his duties under the law.

The aggressiveness of newspapers and the reticence of administrative bodies, especially on the local level, have more than once resulted in litigation and petitions concerning the right of access. The records usually are opened, but each case is decided as an isolated instance rather than in terms of a fixed principle applicable to the country as a whole.

Because of the time delay involved (and the resultant loss of news value), newspapers are reluctant to initiate court action to open records. Instead reporters seek cooperation of officials. The Sigma Delta Chi Committee states:

> Because the press does not manufacture most information, and only reports it, the newspaper must have the cooperation of those persons in whose custody the information is to be found.
> That cooperation, in the main, must be freely given. Yet, because of conflicts between the impulses of political self-preservation which naturally rule most persons in public life, and the obligations of the press to print both the good and the bad, that cooperation must be assiduously cultivated.[9]

The most productive method of obtaining record disclosure is not by force but by cooperating with officials and offering a bit of friendship and publicity in return. The committee report warns that the spirit of cooperation does not mean that a newspaper should curry favor of any political regime, but certainly its representatives should conduct themselves in such a way to establish and maintain their respect. Ultimately, this demeanor will open more records than use of legal force.

ADMINISTRATIVE MEMORANDUM

A test case involving student access to records occurred in New Mexico. An attempt was made by two college journalists to obtain and publish a list of faculty salaries at a state-supported university. The New Mexico Supreme Court reversed a lower court order to release the list.[10]

The two writers, staff members of *The Chase,* school newspaper at Eastern New Mexico University in Portales, had gone to court to gain access to the list of a proposed $1.5 million in salaries to be paid by the university. The writers contended that the records were public information and that the state law defining what documents constitute public records was too strict. But in rejecting access the high court supported the narrow interpretation, saying "the list was not a document required by law to be prepared or preserved. It was prepared and used as a matter of administrative convenience."

University officials had contended that the issue was not one of trying to conceal the list, but rather that it was an administrative memorandum and that the Board of Regents did not feel it was public information until the salaries were officially approved.

Ironically, in the decision's aftermath the immediate issue concerning the list's publication was settled in district court when it was read into the court records—which is, by law, a public record.[11]

JUVENILE COURT RECORDS

Of concern to the student press, the high school press in particular, is the question of access to juvenile court records. Ordinarily the names of juvenile offenders are withheld. Some state laws prohibit the disclosure; in other states it is up to the individual juvenile judge whether or not juvenile crime information is to be released. The rationale behind name withholding is that publicity is thought to hinder, rather than aid, the rehabilitation of juvenile delinquents and the prevention of crime among young people.

The point at which a young person ceases to be a juvenile and becomes an adult (at least in court record terms) depends on juvenile jurisdiction in the individual states. In most states juvenile jurisdiction continues through the 18th year—that is, up to the 18th birthday.

STUDENT ATTENDANCE AT BOARD MEETINGS

Meetings of school boards and state university trustees across the nation vary widely in openness to public scrutiny. "Some

take seemingly extreme measures to prevent the transactions of
these state institutions from being known even to the administrative staffs of the institutions involved."[12]

That is one of the findings of a study by Richmond Brown
of the University of Missouri. Brown found evidence of openness
too. Some boards seem to cultivate public interest in solving academic problems, but "there is a hint that some presidents use in-
timidation to keep students and faculty away from trustees' meetings in spite of open meeting laws, while others give lip service
to freedom of information while meeting in conference rooms
which will not accommodate more than a few guests."[13]

Brown sees a trend toward greater student scrutiny and involvement on boards as well as strong movements for change. The
student reporter in both college and high school should check
on his individual school situation concerning whether he has
standing to attend meetings. Certainly the legal precedent and
legal principle are on his side.

THE POLICE

Municipal and state laws concerning disclosure of police records vary so greatly that generalizations about them are difficult.
As usually defined, police records about investigations in progress
are not considered public; they are instead office memos. Access to
records of this type is by courtesy and is not a common law or
statutory right.[14]

Records of arrests are a different matter. According to most
laws these are considered open to public view. It is presumed
there that the investigatory process has been completed.

One court held that police cannot discriminate between one
type of press and another in releasing information: a police department cannot refuse access to records requested by underground news reporters if it furnishes the same records to the "established" press.[15] Presumably the same nondiscrimination rule
would hold for school-sponsored publications.

Other problems concerning standing have arisen relating to
discriminatory issuance of police passes to members of the commercial press vis-à-vis the student press. The problem occurs primarily in metropolitan areas where public officials and press reporters are less likely to be acquainted. The experience of one
student reporter pinpoints the problem.

Marty Yant was a reporter for the *Voice*, a student newspaper
at Georgetown University, Washington, D.C. He was arrested

while covering an off-campus protest meeting. As he recalls: "As
I attempted to leave, as ordered, I was grabbed from behind by
an officer who refused to listen to my protests that I was with the
press. The policeman refused even to consider the validity of
my press card and threw it and my notes to the ground."[16]

Yant's press badge was an unofficial one, given to him by
Georgetown's Office of Public Relations in hopes that it would
offer him at least some protection. The PR office was unsuccessful
in obtaining press passes from the Washington police department.

As a result of this experience, Arthur Ciervo, director of the
Georgetown PR office, surveyed police chiefs in fifteen large cities.
He found that seven cities do not issue police press passes to campus journalists, five do, and three were noncommital. Ciervo
noted:

> Denial of police press passes to campus journalists is
> certainly discriminatory and presupposes on the part of
> the police departments that students are not entitled to the
> same treatment accorded reporters and editors working for
> the commercial press.[17]

Refusals were based on two arguments: (1) that student journalists were not full-time members of the working press, and (2)
they do not cover off-campus events on a routine basis. These
arguments relate, of course, to the question of standing of the student journalist. Ciervo indicated that the refusal arguments were
archaic. Student newspapers have been covering more and more
off-campus events—reporting legislative meetings, demonstrations,
and other events to student audiences who are increasingly concerned and aware of public events and affairs.

An ironic footnote to the Georgetown affair is that later the
director of the campus radio station obtained White House
press credentials but still could not obtain credentials from the
Washington police department.[18]

SUMMARY

Although most states have open meetings and open records
laws, from a practical standpoint gaining access to such material
depends greatly on reporter enterprise and public official cooperation. Some ethical principles involved: (1) Material that is
obviously an office memorandum is not a public record and

should not be published. (2) Names of first offender juveniles should not be published. (3) Details of police investigations in progress are not considered public.

Legal principle and legal precedent are on the side of the student reporter who wishes to cover a college board of trustees meeting or a community school board meeting. In practice, however, such attendance and reporting are recent developments. Consequently, it is wise for the student to politely and tactfully inform the board of his new-found standing.

CHAPTER EIGHT

SEPARATE PUBLISHING GROUPS

IN MOST HIGH SCHOOLS the question of who has the legal responsibility as publisher of the school newspaper, magazine, or yearbook rarely arises. It is generally understood, either explicitly or implicitly, that the school (that is, the school board) is the "owner" of the publication. The school provides the facilities, pays the supervisor's salary, and often provides equipment and supplies; as long as things roll along smoothly, the publisher aspect is mutually understood. But come the infrequent crisis—a libel suit or publication of a lottery advertisement—then there may be scurrying to find the publication's legal owner. In the settling dust the owner is invariably found to be the school board; and, whether his name is printed on the masthead or not, the high school principal usually performs the functions of a "publisher."[1]

The effort to determine a publication's legal owner arises more often in colleges and universities and with more varying results. Organization and control are more varied, ranging from direct administrative supervision to a phenomenon called the "separate corporation."

TRADITIONAL FORMS

Most high school publications are organized according to direct administrative control. Authority flows (either explicitly or understood) from the publication's legal owner (school board) down the organizational structure to the principal, to the adviser, to the student editors. Within this structure the school newspaper often serves as a laboratory newspaper and is used not only as a medium for dissemination of news and information and as an outlet for student expression but also as an element in classroom instruction in journalism.

Other traditional forms are in varying degrees integrated with or segregated from administrative and/or faculty control. These usually have been structured to fit peculiar or unique community or school situations.

THE LABORATORY NEWSPAPER

Whether in the high school or college or university, the newspaper operating as a laboratory newspaper—a part of classroom instruction—adheres to a rigid control system. Where the material written for the student newspaper is also graded for academic credit, the authoritarian control by faculty and administration is of necessity less flexible than if the paper is completely extracurricular. Although the laboratory newspaper usually is distributed as a student publication, there is an adult authority figure grading the work and supervising the business aspects (although, as previously indicated, this may not be explicitly stated).

Among the problems arising under the strict form are friction and unpleasantness when a principal or dean must rule on a policy decision. Sometimes his ruling constitutes a form of censorship of student work. If the administrator is open-minded and wishes to grant maximum student freedom, his task may be even more unpleasant; he may wish he could rule himself out of the organizational structure.

INTEGRATED-SEGREGATED FORMS

Various forms of integrated and/or segregated approaches, unhampered by usual measures inherent in direct control, have been suggested. Some have been devised to fit unique situations at colleges or universities. One devised at Northern Illinois University involved duplication of prepared news stories—one copy to be used in journalism instruction and another copy to be used for consideration for inclusion in the student newspaper.[2] The most popular form under the integrated-segregated heading involves establishment of an intermediary "board of publications." This form has been used for many years in colleges and universities and is considered a traditional form there; in high schools the board of publications arrangement is more recent.

Board of Publications Approach

A good discussion of the board of publications approach for high schools is contained in an article by Robert Trager and Ron Ostman.[3] It is suggested as a setup which might alleviate the principal's disagreeable duty as censor as well as a means to mitigate other administration-student conflicts. Trager and Ostman offer guidelines on organization of a publications board on the high school level. Bylaws should include statements of policy and goals; composition of the board; duties and responsibilities of the officers and the board; and steps for appointing, reviewing, and removing editors and key staff members. In addition, Trager and Ostman stress that the bylaws should carefully spell out other areas of legitimate concern to the board: approving the budget and financial relationships as well as procedures for hearing and acting upon complaints and compliments.

In a similar set of suggestions, but directed primarily to college and university administrators, Orley R. Herron and Edward E. Ericson[4] emphasize that the nature of student publications must be understood before embarkation on the board of publications route. Their guidelines include these principles:

1. Student publications are not public relations pieces. They are not written to present the picture of the college that the administration holds or wants presented to the public.

2. Student newspapers are not merely a calendar or chronicle of activities on the campus. They should not be limited to straight news reporting any more than a city newspaper is so limited.

3. Student publications are to be the vehicles for the representation of the student mind. This must include experimentation with the expression of new and original ideas.

In setting up the board's physical structure, Herron and Ericson recommend that the majority should be students and a minority administrators and faculty members. If this is done, the publication remains a "student" one and yet students are not deprived of counsel and experience of veterans of the academic community when difficult decisions must be made.

Once the publications board is constituted, the bylaws should be adhered to. The established machinery should not be by-passed. *In no case should there be a direct confrontation between a trustee (or school board member) and a student editor or faculty adviser.*

Another admonition stressed by Herron and Ericson: The administrator should not interrupt the circulation of the student publication except on legal counsel (that is, if a legal counsel advises that an issue contains a libel). It is desirable that student publications reflect good taste, but it is up to the student editors (with counsel from faculty advisers) to determine whether or not the canons of good taste are violated.

What is included in the policies to govern a student board of publications will vary according to philosophy of the situation, the community, and the people preparing the bylaws. Some guidelines on the college level do not give advisers privilege of seeing copy before it reaches print; others do. But certainly on the high school level it makes sense to state in the duties and responsibilities section that the adviser should see news and feature copy before it reaches print, otherwise there is no opportunity for him to advise or instruct.

Most publication board bylaws set up procedures for naming and removing editors and other key staff members. At one school the procedures were not strictly followed and provided an illustration of what happens when the established machinery is by-passed or ignored. This occurred at Wichita State University in 1970 where the publications board was criticized in the student newspaper, the *Sunflower*. The editorial statement recommended that the board of publications be abolished because it was not fulfilling its objectives. It would never meet to decide anything positive, only to decide negatively—such as to remove a staff member. The editorial called for establishment of an independent nonprofit corporation comprised of journalism students, *Sunflower* staff, and an adviser hired by the *Sunflower* to act as publisher.[5] In short, dissatisfied with a loosely organized board of publications, the *Sunflower* proposed a separate corporation.

SEPARATE INCORPORATION

At the high school level, administration-sanctioned newspapers have not moved off campus or become financially independent. Although Robert Glessing estimates that at one time or another there have been 3,000 regularly and irregularly published high school newspapers,[6] these are not "establishment" sanctioned papers maintaining official attachment to the school.

At the college and university level, though, the "separate corporation" has been around for quite some time. The oldest separate corporation structure is that at the University of Illinois where the *Daily Illini* was incorporated in 1911.[7] Over the years several other schools have followed this path: Yale, Dartmouth, and Harvard are among the older ones.

The corporation at Harvard is typical of the older corporations. The Harvard *Crimson,* with a circulation of 5,000, is published daily except Sunday. It is primarily an undergraduate newspaper and is self-supporting from advertising and subscription income totaling $150,000 annually. Its 75 staff members are divided among news, editorial, photo, and business boards. An executive board of 10 senior editors is the final authority, but editorial policies are voted on by all news and editorial personnel, usually about 30. Editors are "nominated" by the retiring board and "ratified" by the entire staff.[8]

The drift toward incorporation of college and university newspapers is increasing; the tendency is away from administration and faculty control. In the two years 1970–71 several more newspapers (by mutual agreement with the schools involved) became separately incorporated—at Indiana University, Boston College, University of Minnesota, University of North Carolina, University of Colorado, Purdue University, Utica College, University of California at Berkeley, University of Iowa, and others. The movement included both private and publicly supported schools.[9] Yearbooks and other publications, though, are seldom separately incorporated.

Impetus for the gravitation toward separate incorporation stems partly from student desire to become assertive and partly from a desire of administrators to be relieved of embarrassment caused by types of material published in school papers during the problem years 1968–69. In addition, the incorporation movement received a boost from the prestigious Association of American University Professors (AAUP), which stated that "whenever possible the student newspaper should be a separate corporation, financially and legally separate from the university."[10]

UNIVERSITY OF NORTH CAROLINA

Most corporations at universities are formed only after a blue-ribbon committee makes an extensive study of the publication situation and then recommends the separate structure. At the University of North Carolina a seven-man committee went beyond a simple answer to a complex question and issued recommendations concerning a wide range of considerations concerning the campus newspaper, the *Tar Heel*.[11] The committee, headed by journalism professor John B. Adams, issued a 7,000-word report dealing with considerations involved and offering guidelines.

One point of contention concerned whether or not compulsory student fees could continue to be collected to help support the newspaper.[12] The committee recommended continuation of fees for a while but favored eventual elimination of fees in favor of chief financial support from advertising. Because the fees are set by the university's board of trustees, the committee thought there was a coercive danger.

The Adams committee recommended establishment of the position of general manager for publications "from the ranks of experienced newsmen" who would serve to provide continuity in the business operations of the publications and who would be available for consultation in journalistic problems "at the initiative of the student journalist."[13] The committee also recommended that the university establish a competitive campus journal to disseminate its own official statements, pronouncements, news of appointments, "and other items of interest to the University and the State." The committee indicated that chances of conflict would be lessened if the administration would not count on the *Tar Heel* to publish such documents verbatim.

PURDUE

Another university that experienced control difficulties resulting in appointment of a high-level investigating committee was Purdue. The difficulties arose in 1968 following publication in the *Exponent* of a column and a poem containing "certain words considered inappropriate in responsible newspapers."[14] Acting outside established procedures, the university president fired the student editor but was forced to rescind his action when it was pointed out that he had not adhered to due process. Thereupon the president requested that a committee of eight professors and administrators and five students be named to make recommendations.

The committee, following a two-month study, recommended a separate nonprofit, nonstock corporation for the *Exponent*. A complicating factor (illustrating that each corporation must be formed on its own merits and in the context of its own community and financial situation) was that a university-related foundation held a mortgage on the newspaper's press, office, and production equipment: value $72,000. In the resulting corporation contract between the university's Board of Trustees and the *Exponent* a lease-purchase arrangement was worked out. The publishing corporation also agreed to pay standard rental for use of 5,500 sq. ft. of space in a university building, where previously the rental had been only token—$33 per year.

In recommending the separate corporation the faculty-student committee sought to place responsibility for success of the newspaper, both financially and editorially, squarely on the corporation. Accordingly, they recommended a student majority on a board of nine. This "predominantly student input" would assist the editor in determining the character and limits of the paper's constituency. The implication: the more the harmony with readership audience, the greater the corporation's chance for success.[15]

FLORIDA

The issue of control also arose in the case involving abortion referral advertising in the University of Florida *Alligator* (see Chapter 5). The battle was on when the paper's editor proposed to publish referral lists, thus violating a 103-year-old state statute. Approved by the Board of Student Publications, the proposal was vetoed by University President Stephen O'Connell. A test case ensued when the lists were distributed anyway, but in mimeographed form, and the statute was eventually overturned.[16]

The battle left scars relating to policy control. President O'Connell sought to clarify and strengthen his authority. He asked the Board of Regents to approve a plan that would allow him to appoint a "professional editor-publisher" responsible to the vice-president for student affairs. Later, when this plan was rejected by the Board of Regents, the president proposed to make the paper completely independent of the university. This was effected, and the paper was ordered to vacate the campus August 31, 1973.[17]

THE SMALL COLLEGE

The movement toward the separate corporation has not been confined to large universities. In 1969 Ithaca College (Ithaca,

N.Y.) established a corporation (see Appendix F for framework and guidelines) which could be used as a model for a possible high school separate corporation. The *Ithacan* was incorporated on approval of the college's Board of Trustees. This paper prints about 25 times each year and maintains a circulation of about 4,500. All corporation officers are students, with an advisory board of both students and nonstudents. With the advisory board the corporation hopes to involve both faculty and residents of the community who are experienced in business, printing, and writing.

The student control board at Ithaca takes full responsibility for all information and editorial material printed in the paper. The administration, under the agreement, neither assigns an adviser nor assumes responsibility for *Ithacan* content.

OTHER REASONS FOR SEPARATE INCORPORATION

In addition to general financial and editorial considerations for separation, there is a legal advantage, at least from the school's viewpoint. If the school is separate from the newspaper, there is less chance the school will be held liable in the event of a legal suit. This cannot be stated positively, because only one university (Vanderbilt) has successfully defended a position of being separate from its publications, and there is some doubt as to whether a legal precedent of liability immunity has been set (see Chapter 2).

A body of legal opinion states that even if the publishing corporation is separate, the parent (school) is still in a position to exercise a substantial degree of control over the subsidiary (publishing corporation). Viewed in this way, the separate publishing corporation is a "legal fiction."[18]

The test of immunity, then, is not settled law. An uncertainty exists concerning the extent to which a court will respect a separate corporation if the school exercises any substantial degree of control over the paper, and it may well depend on the facts of the individual case. If it can be proved that the publication is independent to a great degree in financing and sponsorship (as in the Vanderbilt case), the school would not be legally responsible.

Because a high school has more of an *in loco parentis* aura, it would seem that there would be more difficulty in proving to a court that a separate high school newspaper corporation sanctioned by the school was completely independent.

ADVANTAGES AND DISADVANTAGES

When a group receives a charter from a state to incorporate, it receives certain business advantages. A corporation is an entity created by the state and thus is an artificial personality with a life during the term of its charter. One advantage of the "artificial person" is that transfer of control is flexible—important when editors and staff are transient, in residence for only a few years. Control from one staff to another can be passed along smoothly.

Other benefits can also be gained because the corporation can own property; sell property, goods, and services; hire and fire; sue people; and enter into legal business contracts. To some extent it can stand between the incorporators and the people who want to collect libel damages or bills.

But there also are disadvantages. The corporation must comply with rigorous federal and state regulations, and these require detailed reports at frequent intervals. The extra amount of paperwork is heavy and requires business and statistical acumen. If the staff cannot comply, it may find it necessary to hire an accountant.

There are other pitfalls which may constrain would-be incorporators. For one thing, to remain in operation, the corporation must make its own way financially. Gone is any onus of protection from the administration, or, for that matter, any financial bailing out. Neither is there an intermediary authority available in case of editorial trouble. In a separate corporation a board of directors has the power—and the responsibility—to remove the editor summarily. The board does not even need a good excuse. So there is no more blackmailing of administrators by threats of newspaper activities in order for an editor to keep his job.[19]

Another problem concerns business expertise. Printing contracts can become complicated and circulation practices must be expert and dependable. Incorporation by itself will not pull a paper out of these practical thickets.

Louis J. Berman, *Michigan State News* adviser, indicates there can be a spread of at least 33 percent between high and low bids on the same kind of printing work. This does not necessarily mean that the top bid is crooked and the bottom bid is the best one: there may be extra services involved not reflected in the price. Berman states:

> One of the important things about newspaper publishing is that you have to be able to get your paper out when you say you will. If you're late too often, you'll lose

readers and you'll lose advertisers. So one of the *must* requirements in picking a printer is to be sure your publication will get the VIP treatment it needs to come out on time.[20]

In circulation, decisions must be made whether or not to try for a regular fee per student per semester or quarter; to try the voluntary subscription method; or to go for free circulation. Each has benefits and drawbacks, and the decision—related of course to what can be offered to advertisers and to freedom from student government control—must be expert and businesslike if the paper is to survive.

THE ADMINISTRATION PAPER

One result of the growing disassociation of student newspapers from college and university ties is the growth of free-distribution weekly and biweekly newssheets published and supported by administrations. Such papers have been established at Cornell, Stanford, Purdue, Pennsylvania State, Columbia, and Boston universities.

For the most part the newssheets are produced by university news services and concentrate on reporting events rather than issues and problems. Bill Ward, reporting on the growth in numbers of such papers, writes that they perform functions that student-edited newspapers formerly handled. "Once the student press curtailed its role as a public relations instrument, administrators sought a new tool—and have found it."[21]

The newssheets are, for the most part, information-centered. They do such things as explain the official university position and endeavor to present a positive image of the campus to students and the outside community.

Ward believes that in performing these functions, the administration papers might possibly become competitors with the independent student newspapers.

SUMMARY

At high schools the movement for separate incorporation has not begun. Instead the situation has been that when the official high school paper becomes unacceptable, students have moved to establish underground publications. There is no record of any high school underground paper ever having received a corporate charter.

Separate incorporation is gaining in popularity at the college and university level. The structures that have evolved are varied. Some corporations have remained on campus, with administrative sanction; others, with sanction, have moved off campus. Those who desire a separate publishing corporation should talk the matter over with the school attorney. Degrees of financial and editorial freedom under the corporate form may vary depending on individual school and community relationships.

Motivation for separate incorporation has come not only from students and the staffs of student publications but also from administrators who tire of explaining student newspaper actions to their constituent groups. With divorce the legal and financial relationships become more clear.

Some advantages accrue to a corporation formed within a state: the publishing corporation becomes autonomous in its business practices. But there are disadvantages and pitfalls: more forms dealing with fiscal accountability and a requirement for practical business expertise.

But under the corporate form the paper can be responsible, possibly even more so than under some form of paternalistic system. If the paper covers campus news, it will have readership; if it has readership, it will have ads; if it has ads, the staff and the printer will be paid; and payment means that another paper will be issued. A responsible newspaper can keep up with all these aspects.

CHAPTER NINE

OFF-CAMPUS DISTRIBUTION

✄

SCHOOL OFFICIALS FACE several problems when they try to balance the right to distribute student publications with the need to maintain school order (see Chapter 1). City officials face many of the same problems when they attempt to regulate distribution of periodicals in public places. On the one hand, the Constitution guarantees freedom of the press, a freedom that includes the right of distribution. On the other, this freedom must be subject to the requirements of an orderly society. The press is not free of "the ordinary restraints and regulations of the modern state" (*Breard* v. *Alexandria,* 341 U.S. 622).

Courts do not always agree on what restraints and regulations are reasonable, but the U.S. Supreme Court has ruled that when a city licensing scheme results in prior censorship of the press, it is constitutionally prohibited (*Schneider* v. *New Jersey,* 308 U.S. 147). Hence many municipal licensing ordinances do not hold up under legal challenge. The challengers often are underground newspaper distributors, whose legal rights to freedom of speech and the press are no different from those of other citizens.

OUTRIGHT BANS

Any outright ban on the sale of newspapers undoubtedly is unconstitutional. In 1966 staff members of the underground *Columbia Free Press* at the University of Missouri successfully protested to city officials when the sale of the newspaper was banned in Columbia. A city ordinance prohibited the sale of merchandise on any street or sidewalk and was interpreted to include the *Free Press*. The students first circumvented the ordinance by giving away the publication and soliciting contributions in return. A few months later the Columbia City Council amended the ordinance to allow the sale of newspapers and pamphlets on city property.[1]

OBSCENITY

Arrests of underground newspaper distributors often are made for alleged violations of obscenity laws, since obscenity is not constitutionally protected. Normally officials may not simply seize copies of a newspaper without a search warrant or prior hearing to determine obscenity.[2] Also, many obscenity laws are unenforceable and charges are often dismissed.

When the Boston *Avatar* repeatedly used offensive words in issues being distributed near Harvard, the paper's salesmen were arrested a total of 58 times by Cambridge police. A local court found the words not obscene, and the *Avatar* reached a truce with city officials by agreeing to stop sales to anyone under 18.[3]

PERMITS

Some cities require newspaper salesmen to obtain distribution permits. But when a permit can be denied or revoked simply at the discretion of administrative officers, an ordinance will not be upheld in court.

In the fall of 1969 four salesmen of the underground newspaper *Extra* were arrested in Providence, Rhode Island, and charged with working as newsboys without permits. A city ordinance required newspaper salesmen to register with the bureau of licenses to obtain permits, which could be refused if applicants were not of "good character." A permit could also be revoked if a salesman was caught using profane language or if he became guilty of disorderly conduct. Each salesman had to deposit 50 cents for a numbered badge to wear on his hat or cap.

Members of the *Extra* staff brought suit, charging that licensing of newsboys was a violation of constitutional free press guarantees.[4] A U.S. District Court found the Providence ordinance "unconstitutional as an impermissible direct restraint upon freedom of the press and as a licensing scheme which vests overly broad and vague discretionary powers in the chief of police and members of the licensing bureau." The decision seemed to turn on the fact that the police chief had to make a recommendation

on the "good character" of an applicant before the licensing
bureau could grant the permit, not on the fact that a permit was
required.

The U.S. Court of Appeals in Boston upheld the district
court's ruling and also found that the physical acts of registration
and procuring a badge could not be constitutionally required.
Said the court:

> If we were to find this permissible, plaintiffs would be
> required to open themselves to possible identification as
> the ones associated with *Extra,* to deposit fifty cents with
> the city, and possibly to suffer the felt stigma of having to
> display a button. . . . We therefore hold these require-
> ments of the ordinance, like its other provisions, unconsti-
> tutional.

POSTING BONDS

Requiring a newspaper salesman to post a large bond to obtain a peddler's permit is a possible violation of free press guarantees.

On June 7, 1971, the City Council of West Lafayette, Indiana, quietly amended a 1956 peddler's ordinance. Before the
amendment it was relatively easy to obtain a peddler's permit
on application. After the amendment a peddler had to post a
$1,000 bond to obtain a permit. Exempted from the bonding re-
quirement were those who had been in business in the city or
county during the preceding twelve months.

On September 13, 1971, two salesmen of *Red Brick,* a new
underground newspaper at Purdue University, were arrested on
a city street and charged with selling without a permit. The
Lafayette *Journal and Courier,* the area's commercial newspaper,
called the bonding requirement "an illegal harassment of young
and unconventional publishers" and "an inequitable shackle on
the poor."[5] A city councilman denied that the ordinance was
directed at any one group, maintaining that it was enacted "to
protect our citizens against the questionable practices of some
peddlers and salesmen who visit our city."[6] After Purdue students and the American Civil Liberties Union protested, charges
against *Red Brick* salesmen were dropped and the city council
revised the ordinance. The bonding requirement was eliminated
and the sale of single copies of newspapers was allowed with no
requirement that salesmen register with police. Those who sold

printed matter "on contract" (by subscription) and who had lived in the county for less than one year still had to register with the police, but no bond was involved.[7]

SUSPENSION FROM SCHOOL

Even though underground newspaper distributors may not be breaking local laws, they can still run into trouble with school authorities.

In *Baker* v. *Downey City Board of Education*,[8] a California court upheld a high school's right to suspend students who were distributing an underground newspaper near the campus. The newspaper, *Oink*, contained profanity and was critical of school officials. The students were suspended under the authority of the California Education Code, which stated, in part:

> Continued willful disobedience, habitual profanity or vulgarity . . . at any time or place shall constitute good cause for suspension or expulsion from school; however, no pupil shall be suspended or expelled unless the conduct for which he is to be disciplined is related to school activity or school attendance.

A U.S. District Court ruled that "school authorities are responsible for the morals of the students while going to and from school, as well as during the time they are on campus." Furthermore,

> the fact the distribution was technically not on campus because the paper was handed to students just outside the main gate does not mitigate against the fact that plaintiffs knew the students were entering the campus for class and also knew and intended that *Oink* would be well distributed on campus.

If an underground newspaper distributed off-campus is not profane, libelous, or inflammatory and is no threat to the operation of the school, a court might take a different view.

In *Shanley* v. *Northeast Independent School District*,[9] the U.S. Court of Appeals for the Fifth Circuit overruled Texas school officials who had suspended five students from San Antonio's MacArthur High School for distributing an underground newspaper near the school. The newspaper, *Awakening*, advocated a review of the laws on smoking marijuana and listed the phone number of a clinic offering birth control and venereal disease information. School officials considered *Awakening* potentially disruptive and suspended student distributors under the authority of a district policy forbidding "the distribution of petitions or printed documents of any kind, sort, or type without the specific approval of the principal."

The court noted that publications produced by students can be subject to prior screening "under clear and reasonable regulations" but the district's policy was unconstitutionally overbroad

> (1) because it purports to establish a prior restraint on any and all exercise of expression by means of the written word on the part of high school students at any time and in any place for any reason; and (2) because it contains no standards whatsoever by which principals might guide their administrative screenings of "petitions or printed documents of any kind, sort, or type."

The court observed that *Awakening* was written and distributed by students before and after school without any use of school facilities, nothing in the newspaper was illegal, the newspaper was distributed in a polite and orderly fashion, and distributors even discouraged other students from taking the paper on school grounds. Moreover, the court emphasized that there were no disruptions in connection with *Awakening* and no evidence that the newspaper could have interfered with school operations. In the absence of such evidence the school had no legal right to punish the students. The court ordered the school to clear the students' records and give them the opportunity to make up missed work.

SUMMARY

Any city licensing scheme that results in prior censorship of the press is constitutionally prohibited. Hence many municipal licensing ordinances do not hold up under legal challenge by underground newspaper distributors.

City officials usually may not seize copies of a publication thought to be obscene without a search warrant or a prior hearing to determine obscenity.

When a distribution permit can be denied or revoked simply at the discretion of an administrative officer, an ordinance will not be upheld in court.

Requiring newspaper distributors to post a large bond to obtain a distribution permit is a possible violation of constitutional free press guarantees.

Even though underground newspaper distributors may not be breaking local laws, they may still be disciplined by school officials. In some states a student may be expelled or suspended for distributing libelous, inflammatory, or profane publications off school grounds if his conduct is related to school attendance or activity.

CHAPTER TEN

SELECTED PROBLEMS

OTHER LEGAL PROBLEMS confronting school administrators, publication advisers, and student journalists involve the areas of privacy rights, tax exemptions, student broadcasting, and postal regulations.

PRIVACY

A picture of a two-year-old girl appeared in the Vanderbilt University humor magazine, the *Chase,* in 1954. The picture had been sent to the printer two years before for use in a family's Christmas cards, and through a mixup the same photograph appeared in a *Chase* layout which poked fun at Mother's Day. As a result, the father of the girl filed six suits against the university for libel and invasion of privacy.

The father charged that the picture, used without his permission, implied that his daughter was interested in illicit sexual intercourse and the magazine feature placed her in an extremely embarrassing and false position. As it turned out, the suits against the magazine were not pressed, but instead new suits were brought against the Vanderbilt student newspaper, the *Hustler,* for its story of the pleadings (see Chapter 2). However, publication of the *Chase* was discontinued by the university after the incident. The problems encountered by the magazine illustrate what can happen if a student publication is charged with invading someone's privacy.

The right of privacy is the right to be let alone, to live one's life without being subjected to unwanted publicity. The right is not an absolute, however. Public officials give up many of their privacy rights since it is in the public interest that voters know about their activities. Private citizens who become involved in a public event (for example, an automobile accident) usually cannot avoid publicity. Still, the courts have recognized that every citizen has the right to withhold some of his activities from public view and to protect himself against improper use of his name or photograph.

Many student publications are so carefully controlled that they do not illegally invade a person's privacy. But there are two areas in which they might inadvertently violate privacy laws: (1) placing someone in an extremely embarrassing situation or in a false position, and (2) using a person's name or photograph in an advertisement without his consent.

As in the Vanderbilt case, placing a person in an extremely embarrassing or false position can result in suits for both libel and invasion of privacy. Also, attributing views to someone that he may not hold can result in action on right of privacy grounds, since this is putting a person in a false light.

A person's name and picture may be used in a news story without his permission as long as the story is of timely interest to readers. However, written consent should be obtained when a name or photograph is used in an advertisement. In the case of a minor, the consent should come from a parent. This is not a hard and fast rule, however. If a student volunteers to appear in an advertisement and if no embarrassment would result, it is probable that no action for invasion of privacy would be brought against the school by the student's parents.

TAXATION

As discussed in the chapter on separate corporations, several college and university newspapers have become independent in recent years. In going independent, however, some have retained partial educational ties. The Harvard *Crimson,* long an independent corporation, has continued federal tax-exempt status as a nonprofit educational organization. So has the Columbia University *Daily Spectator.*[1] To maintain tax exemption according to the U.S. Internal Revenue code, however, a publication must not endorse political candidates.[2]

A test of the regulation came in 1970–71. An Internal Revenue district director in New York City questioned the *Spectator*'s qualifications for exempt status. The contention: In 1966 and 1968 the newspaper had "endorsed" political candidates in its editorial columns, including Nelson Rockefeller for governor and Eldridge Cleaver for president.

The *Spectator* countered by claiming the editorials did not constitute endorsements. For example, a 1966 editorial concluded: "Mr. Rockefeller has made an adequate Governor. He could make a very good one indeed. Neither of his opponents is likely to do better."[3]

The resulting Internal Revenue review was the first of its kind involving the tax-exempt section of the code. In June 1971 the decision was announced: "In the context of relevant facts" the *Spectator* was not in violation of code provisions. The paper could keep its tax-exempt status.[4]

The IRS gave no reason for its decision, but in a significant fact sheet attached to the ruling the IRS noted that the Spectator Publishing Company's paper's editorials were often followed by notes that one or more individual editors dissented from the views expressed. Presumably, the IRS believed that the *Spectator*'s editorials stopped short of the degree of endorsement necessary to revoke its tax-exempt status. Also, IRS noted that the *Spectator* ruling applied only to that newspaper. It cautioned against broad interpretation.[5]

If its tax exemption had been revoked, the *Spectator* would have had to pay up to $9,000 per year for its office space at Columbia.[6]

Some administrators, with tax exemption in mind, issue protective guidelines to college-controlled publications concerning political endorsements. Chancellor Glenn S. Dumke of the California State College system advised San Jose State's *Spartan Daily* editors to discuss issues editorially and not endorse candidates.[7]

Another decree appeared as an overreaction to the *Spectator* review. The administration at St. John's University, a private school at Jamaica, New York, issued a policy statement to dissociate the university from the 1970 election campaigns. The student newspaper, the *Downtowner,* was admonished not "to print editorials, feature stories, signed columns or letters to the editor that in any way deal with the political campaigns." The university saw "no problem with straight news stories." The statement added, however, that if political news stories appeared, the university would not mail the *Downtowner* off campus.[8]

When the paper's staff objected to the university's squelching "several constitutional freedoms in its attempt to cover itself on one IRS regulation," the St. John's president reacted by suggesting that the student newspaper could "get the hell off campus" because otherwise the university was responsible for it. In its final word the university stated it would stand on its guidelines and insist that any violation would be between the *Downtowner* and the IRS.[9]

There is an indication that the IRS political endorsement policy also extends to high school newspapers.[10]

In sum, each tax exemption case would be decided on its merits. No blanket policy has been articulated.

BROADCASTING

Noncommercial educational broadcasting stations are licensed by the Federal Communications Commission (FCC) and, like commercial stations, are required to operate in "the public interest, convenience, and necessity."[11] Educational stations must comply with the Communications Act of 1934 as amended, the Public Broadcasting Act of 1967, the rules and regulations of the FCC, and the broadcast provisions of the U.S. Criminal Code (see Appendices G and H).

Student organizations normally are not awarded broadcast licenses. The FCC usually wants assurances that there will be faculty supervision and control, and grants a license only to the governing body of a high school or college. The legal responsibilities accompanying a license cannot be delegated by the license holder, and failure to meet these responsibilities can result in a station losing its license or even in legal action.

The U.S. Criminal Code prohibits the broadcast of obscene, profane, or indecent language and makes those who utter or permit the utterance of such language subject to a $10,000 fine and a two-year prison sentence (18 U.S.C. 1464). Although seldom enforced, the law gives school officials grounds to act against students who use or permit the use of such language on the air. In 1970, after radio station WCWP-FM at private C. W. Post College in New York broadcast objectionable language, the station director was removed from his position and the station was temporarily closed by college officials. The station director and student and faculty listeners then brought suit, maintaining that the college violated the First and Fourteenth Amendments in that it deprived listeners of the right to receive information and ideas.[12]

A U.S. District Court did not agree, saying that neither state nor federal involvement had been demonstrated in the case and noting that only governmental action can violate the First and Fourteenth Amendments. The college was held to be a "private entity, acting neither in behalf of, nor as agents for, the Federal Government." The court ruled: "To hold that the licensing by the Federal Government of a broadcast frequency endows the recipient with the quality of an agency of the Federal Government would be an unreasonable interpretation of governmental action."

Would the decision have been any different had C. W. Post been a public college? The court noted:

> The complaint does not allege, nor does it otherwise appear from the facts pleaded, that the state is in any way involved in the affairs of [the college] much less that the state has so insinuated itself into a position of interdependence with the [college] that the actions of the trustees thereof become "State action."

However, the court said that the government "is not charged with the duty of broadcasting or formulating the program of any particular radio station. In fact, the Communications Act of 1934 exclusively reserves station programming to the licensee."

Most conflicts between administrators and student broadcasters are resolved without legal action. In 1971 students and administrators reached an agreement on the operation of WGTB-FM at Georgetown (D.C.) University and averted total shutdown of the station. The university had ordered the station off the air because its 14,720-watt transmitter was disrupting instruments in a nearby science building. After discussions with students, Georgetown agreed to allow the station to broadcast only during evening hours. Student station manager Peter Chowka charged that the university was primarily interested in not disturbing laser research being conducted in the science building under a Defense Department grant.[13]

POSTAL REGULATIONS

Since many college and university publications are distributed to some extent outside the campus (mail subscriptions, exchanges, etc.), institutions of higher learning often take out second-class mailing permits in order to qualify for lower postal rates. For the small newspaper with little outside circulation and for the high school newspaper, permit bookkeeping vexations often outweigh benefits.

If a publication can qualify, a second-class bulk mailing permit can be obtained from the U.S. Post Office. For a publication with a circulation of 2,000 or less, the cost of the permit is $30. A second-class permit allows items weighing less than one ounce (which can include tabloid newspapers up to eight pages containing 50 percent advertising) to be mailed at a cost of approximately one cent per each three items (based on a hypothetical mail circulation of 400, using rates effective January 1, 1973). A publication with no extensive mail circulation can utilize third-class or first-class mailing at higher rates. One commentator places the mail circulation break at 1,000.[14] This means if the publication's mail circulation is less than 1,000, the financial benefits are negligible; above 1,000 a permit might be worthwhile.

Requirements to secure a second-class mailing permit include a statement of ownership. This should come from a school administrative official. Other requirements: The publication must be regularly issued at stated intervals (at least four times a year), bear a date of issue, be numbered consecutively, and be issued from a known office of publication. In addition, the publication must be formed of printed paper sheets. A paper printed by the offset method would qualify, but a mimeographed one would not. Also the publication "must be originated and published for the purpose of disseminating information of a public character, or . . . must be devoted to literature, the sciences, art, or some special industry."[15] Unless the publication is published by a "regularly incorporated institution of learning," it also must have a list of legitimate subscribers.

The application containing the required information is forwarded by the postmaster at the office of application to the Director, Office of Mail Classification, Bureau of Finance and Administration, who rules on all applications. Before taking action the director may call on the publisher for additional information or evidence to support or clarify the application. Later, if the application is denied, the director must notify the publisher specifying the reasons. If the permit is granted, other requirements must be met, including identification statements (see Appendix J).

The holder of a second-class permit must annually file and publish a statement of ownership. This statement must include the names and addresses of the editor, managing editor, publisher, business manager, and owner. If the publication is owned by a corporation, the names and addresses of all stockholders owning 1 percent or more must be listed. In addition, the statement must list the average number of copies sold or distributed during the preceding 12 months.

The publication's staff should be aware that no advertising or news that features lotteries should be sent through the mails. The Post Office has defined a lottery as a scheme where a consideration is furnished for a prize that is dependent on chance. All three elements—consideration, prize, and chance—must be present if the scheme is to be regarded as a lottery.

Over the years "consideration" has caused the most problems in definition and enforcement.[16] Obviously a cash expenditure to purchase a ticket is consideration, but what about the expenditure of time to register for a ticket? In recent years the interpretation has been this: If a person is required to go to a certain place to register for a drawing and also must be present when the drawing is made, the expenditure of the person's time is deemed "consideration." On the other hand, mere registration of a name alone in order to qualify for a prize is not "consideration"; the expenditure of time in this situation is negligible or nonexistent.

The usual penalty for violation of the lottery law is denial of use of the mails. The postal law provides no exception for lotteries conducted by churches, fraternal groups, or other "worthy organizations." Also, the Post Office indicates that it enforces the national statute uniformly without regard to laws which have been enacted in various states declaring certain games of chance to be permissible.[17]

SUMMARY

There are two areas in which student publications might inadvertently violate privacy laws: (1) placing someone in an extremely embarrassing situation or in a false position, and (2) using a person's name or photograph in an advertisement without his consent.

If tax-exempt student publications endorse candidates for public office, they may lose their tax exemptions.

A license for a noncommercial educational broadcast station

normally is granted only to the governing body of a high school or college. Responsibilities accompanying a license cannot be delegated, and failure to meet these responsibilities can result in legal action.

If a student publication has a regular mailing of 1,000 or more copies, it may be wise to obtain a second-class postage permit. Regardless of which class of mail is used, federal and state laws prohibit the publicizing of lotteries.

APPENDICES

APPENDIX A

JOINT STATEMENT ON THE RIGHTS AND FREEDOMS OF STUDENTS — STUDENT PUBLICATIONS

FROM *AAUP Bulletin,* Summer 1968. The following is part of a statement on student rights drafted by representatives of the American Association of University Professors, U.S. National Student Association, Association of American Colleges, National Association of Student Personnel Administrators, and National Association of Women Deans and Counselors. The statement was subsequently endorsed by the American Association for Higher Education; Jesuit Education Association; American College Personnel Association; Executive Committee, College and University Department, National Catholic Education Association; and Commission on Student Personnel, American Association of Junior Colleges; as well as the five national sponsors.

Student publications and the student press are a valuable aid in establishing and maintaining an atmosphere of free and responsible discussion and of intellectual exploration on the campus. They are a means of bringing student concerns to the attention of the faculty and the institutional authorities and of formulating student opinion on various issues on the campus and in the world at large.

Whenever possible the student newspaper should be an independent corporation financially and legally separate from the university. Where financial and legal autonomy is not possible, the institution, as the publisher of student publications, may have to bear the legal responsibility for the contents of the publications. In the delegation of editorial responsibility to students the institution must provide sufficient editorial freedom and financial autonomy for the student publications to maintain their integrity of purpose as vehicles for free inquiry and free expression in an academic community.

Institutional authorities, in consultation with students and faculty, have a responsibility to provide written clarification of the role of the student publications, the standards to be used in their evaluation, and the limitations on external control of their operation. At the same time, the editorial freedom of student editors and managers entails corollary responsibilities to be governed by the canons of responsible journalism, such as the avoidance of libel, indecency, undocumented allegations, attacks on personal integrity, and the techniques of harassment and innuendo. As safeguards for the editorial freedom of student publications the following provisions are necessary:

1. The student press should be free of censorship and advance approval of copy, and its editors and managers should be free to develop their own editorial policies and news coverage.

2. Editors and managers of student publications should be protected from arbitrary suspension and removal because of student, faculty, administrative, or public disapproval of editorial policy or content. Only for proper and stated causes should editors and managers be subject to removal and then by orderly and prescribed procedures. The agency responsible for the appointment of editors and managers should be the agency responsible for their removal.

3. All university published and financed student publications should explicitly state on the editorial page that the opinions there expressed are not necessarily those of the college, university, or student body.

APPENDIX B

AMERICAN CIVIL LIBERTIES UNION STATEMENT
ON FREEDOM OF THE HIGH SCHOOL PRESS

FROM *The Education Digest,* December 1968. The following is a condensation of a portion of "Academic Freedom in the Secondary Schools," a statement prepared by the Academic Freedom Committee of the American Civil Liberties Union.

Generally speaking, students should . . . be permitted and encouraged to produce such publications as they wish. Faculty advisors should serve as consultants on format and suitability of the materials, but neither they nor the principal should prohibit the publication or distribution of material except when the health and safety of students or the educational process are threatened, or the material might be of a libelous nature. Such judgment, however, should never be exercised because of disapproval or disagreement with the article in question.

The administration and faculty should ensure that students and faculty may have their views represented in the school newspaper, and where feasible, should permit multiple and competing periodicals, perhaps produced by existing groups or by individuals banded together for this purpose.

Freedom to express one's opinion goes hand in hand with responsibility for the published statement. The onus of decision on content should be placed clearly on the student editorial board of the publication. The editors should be encouraged through practice to learn to judge literary value, newsworthiness, and propriety.

The student press should be considered a learning device. Its pages should not be looked on as an official image of the school, always required to present a polished appearance. Much may sometimes be learned from reactions to a poor article or a tasteless publication.

Reasonable access to other media, such as the public address system, closed-circuit television, bulletin boards, and handbills, should be afforded to student groups for statements to the school community, as well as space, both indoor and outdoor, for meetings and rallies. The school community, i.e., the administration, faculty, and the student organization, has the right to make reasonable regulations as to manner, place, and time of using these communication media.

APPENDIX C

AMERICAN BAR ASSOCIATION STATEMENT
ON FREEDOM OF THE CAMPUS PRESS

FROM *Chronicle of Higher Education*, February 24, 1970. Part of a statement issued by a study commission of the American Bar Association.

Freedom of the press is in a basic sense but a special aspect of freedom of speech. As a consequence, many of the rules protecting and limiting other modes of expression on campus will apply equally to the regulation of publications.

Ideological censorship is thus to be avoided in the determination of printed matter available on campus; access to publications is not to be denied because of disapproval of their content; and regulation of student publications that operate on the same basis as other private enterprises should be subject only to the same control as those respecting the reasonableness of time, place, and manner of distribution.

Similarly, valid general laws proscribing willful defamation, public obscenity, and other actionable wrongs apply equally to printed matter as to other forms of expression on campus. Finally, just as the institution has an obligation to discourage interference with speech, so also may it prohibit acts of vandalism or other misconduct that seeks to hinder the orderly distribution and availability of publications on campus.

The fact of institutional subsidy and liability does not warrant censorship of editorial policy or content in any broad sense. The university may provide for limited review, however, solely as a reasonable precaution against the publication of matter which would expose the institution to liability.

At the same time, editors and managers of student publications should be protected from arbitrary suspension and removal from office because of student, faculty, or administrative disapproval of editorial policy or content. Only for proper and stated causes should editors and managers be subject to removal and then by orderly and prescribed procedures.

Where the student press is supported by compulsory student fees or other significant university subsidy or where there is a generally accepted public identification with the particular institution, it may properly be subject to rules providing for a right of reply by any person adversely treated in its publication or in disagreement with its editorial policy or its treatment of a given event.

University published and financed student publications should appropriately indicate that the opinions there expressed are not necessarily those of the university or the student body. Moreover, other student publications may fairly be required to indicate that they are not published or financed by the university, and that opinions expressed therein are without university endorsement.

APPENDIX D

High School Newspaper Policy Statement

From *Quill and Scroll*, December 1971-January 1972. The author of this statement is Bert N. Bostrom, assistant professor of journalism at Northern Arizona University, Flagstaff. He offers it as a guide for high school faculty and students who may be in the process of drafting their own statements.

STATEMENT OF POLICY
EAST HIGH SCHOOL GAZETTE

1. The Gazette, while it is a campus newspaper, directed and edited by students, is usually regarded by the public at large as representative not only of the students, but of the faculty, administration and East High School as a whole. The Gazette, therefore, will never be used:

   A) To advance selfish interests of any group or clique of students and/or faculty.

   B) To attack individuals or groups.

   C) To publish any material that is libelous, blasphemous, obscene, or in bad taste. Obscene shall be defined as those so-called four letter words which are avoided in editorial or advertising content in professional, commercial daily or weekly newspapers or what may be considered as obscene by the codes of the Post Office Department.

2. We understand that The Gazette is in no way a free lance publication. We recognize the Board of Education and the school administration as our publisher, and that, in the last analysis, the responsibility for the proper conduct of The Gazette rests with the publisher.

3. We understand that the newspaper editor and staff occupy positions which possess the power to injure individuals and institutions and that our actions at all times will be conditioned by restraint, a strong sense of responsibility, and an extreme care for accuracy.

4. We recognize that our publisher, as a legal entity, may be held liable for injury incurred from actions of members of the staff.

5. In all editorials, in-depth stories, signed letters and other articles which may be considered for publication in The Gazette the following will always be used as guides.

   A) All the pertinent, available facts that can be produced from all sources must be obtained before anything is written or published.

   B) If all the facts cannot be gathered in time to meet a publications deadline, the editorial, in-depth story, signed letter, or other article will be held until such time as that information can be obtained or the copy will not be published at all.

   C) The question of the appropriateness of the time to write or publish the above mentioned articles will be thoughtfully and carefully considered. Counsel will be sought from the adviser and/or school officials involved in each case.

   D) The effect of the above mentioned articles on the school and community will be carefully considered.

   E) All various salient sides of any controversial questions involved in the above mentioned articles will be published in the same issue of the newspaper. It is contrary to the

best ethics of journalism to print one side of the story in
one issue while deferring the other side to a later edition.
6. We recognize that, in many situations, members of the administration are aware of special situations, agreements, and
unusual problems which would not be apparent in even a
professional job of investigation. The counsel of the administration will be sought when any question of this kind may
arise.
7. We accept the philosophy of East High School as a constant
as we plan copy and photographic content for The Gazette.

APPENDIX E

COLLEGE COMMUNICATIONS BOARD CONSTITUTION AND BYLAWS

THE Constitution and Bylaws of the Student Communications Board
of the University of Cincinnati.

CONSTITUTION

ARTICLE I. NAME AND PURPOSE
  Section 1. The name of this organization shall be the Student
  Communications Board of the University of Cincinnati.
  Section 2. The purpose of the Student Communications Board
  shall be to be responsible for the policies of the
  organizations under the jurisdiction of this Board.

ARTICLE II. MEMBERSHIP
  Section 1. The membership of the Student Communications
  Board shall be as follows:
    A. The executive officers of each member organiza-
    tion: Editor of the News Record (campus news-
    paper); Business Manager of the News Record;
    Editor of the Cincinnatian (yearbook); Business
    Manager of the Cincinnatian; Editor of the
    Student Directory; Business Manager of Stu-
    dent Directory; Editor of Profile (literary maga-
    zine); Business Manager of Profile; Editor of
    Draught (humor magazine); Business Manager
    of Draught; General Manager of WFIB (cam-
    pus radio station); Sales Manager of WFIB.
    B. One at-large representative each from the News
    Record, the Cincinnatian, Student Directory,
    Profile, Draught, and WFIB, elected by the
    staffs of the respective groups. At-large repre-

sentatives must be individuals not serving on
the Board in some other capacity.

C. Two representatives from the Student Senate,
appointed by the Student Body president with
advice and consent of the Student Senate.

D. One graduate student representative, appointed
by the Graduate Student Association.

E. A faculty representative, appointed by the Faculty Senate for a term of two years.

F. The Dean of Students or his designee.

G. The University Public Information Officer or
his designee.

H. The Advisers of each member organization to
serve as ex officio members and resource persons
of the Board.

ARTICLE III. APPOINTMENT AND DISMISSAL OF EXEC-
UTIVE OFFICERS

Section 1. Eligibility

Any student meeting the following requirements is
eligible to apply for a position as an executive
officer:

A. He must be a full-time student in good standing at the University of Cincinnati at the time
of application.

B. He must intend to be a full-time student for
the duration of the appointment.

C. He must have a cumulative grade point average of at least 2.3 at the end of the quarter in
which he applies.

Section 2. Appointment of Executive Officers

A. The Student Communications Board shall separately appoint the new executive officers of
each of the member organizations. A simple
majority shall be necessary for appointment.

B. The Board shall appoint persons for the above
positions according to the vote of the following:

1. The editorial (or managerial) executive of
the organization involved. If the representative-at-large is a candidate for an executive position, the representative shall not
have a vote. The staff shall then have 4
votes instead of 3.

2. The financial executive of the organization
involved.

3. The representative-at-large from the organization involved. If the representative-at-
large is a candidate for an executive position, the representative shall not have a
vote. The staff shall then have 4 votes instead of 3.

       4. The two representatives from Student Senate.

       5. The graduate student representative.

       6. The Dean of Students or his designee.*

       7. The Public Information Officer or his designee.*

       8. The faculty representative.

          (The above-named persons must be present at the election meetings.)

          *Designee refers only to a regularly appointed, full-time designee.

       9. The staff of the organization shall have three votes. The staff of the organization involved shall express its choice for executive positions by means of a staff vote.

    C. A student Communications Board member shall not be allowed to vote in an election in which he is one of the candidates.

Section 3. Appointment Approval

    A. The executive officers appointed by the Board shall be subject to the confirmation of the Student Senate.

    B. Newly-appointed officers of member organizations shall appoint their respective staffs. The new staffs shall take office at a time agreed upon by the old and new executives.

Section 4. Dismissal

    A. Any executive officer appointed by the Student Communications Board may be dismissed by the Board for any of the following reasons:

       1. Violation of city and/or state libel and obscenity laws.

       2. Deliberately published or broadcasted falsification.

       3. Neglect of executive or financial responsibilities.

    B. Any action on dismissal of a Board-appointed officer shall be preceded by a hearing with the officer and the Board.

    C. Dismissal must be by a three-quarters majority of the entire Board.

    D. Student Senate may initiate action leading to the possible removal of any Board-appointed officer by making a recommendation for dismissal to the Board.

Section 5. Censorship

    A. The Charter of Student Rights and Responsibilities states that there shall be no censorship of student publications.

Section 6. Censure

    A. The Student Communications Board shall be

empowered by a three-quarter vote of its membership to censure a member organization or an officer thereof.

B. The faculty adviser of each member organization may prohibit that publication or broadcast of any material that is false or libelous. The editorial (or managerial) executive of the organization may request that the Board overrule such decisions by the faculty adviser. The Board must take action within one week in such cases; a two-thirds vote of the Board membership is required to overrule such a decision.

ARTICLE IV. APPOINTMENT AND DISMISSAL OF MEMBERS-AT-LARGE

Section 1. Appointment

A. Following election of executive officers and prior to the next meeting of the Board, a meeting of the new staff of each member organization shall be held to determine members-at-large to the Board. The meeting shall be conducted by the outgoing chairman of the Board. The new editorial (or managerial) and financial officers shall submit a list of staff to the Chairman of the Board; the new executive officers shall not vote.

B. Nominations for the position shall be made from the floor; nominees will have a chance to speak. The selection will be immediately announced.

Section 2. Dismissal

A. A petition, signed by one-fifth of the staff (as determined by the executive officers), will require a vote on the recall of the representative-at-large. Immediately prior to the vote, an open meeting will be held, conducted by a student senator and the faculty adviser of the organization, to allow the representative-at-large to speak to the staff and answer questions.

B. If a representative-at-large is recalled by a two-thirds majority of all staff members, the staff must elect another representative before the next meeting of the Student Communications Board, according to the selection procedures in Section 1 of Article V.

ARTICLE V. OFFICERS OF THE BOARD

Section 1. The officers of the Board shall be Chairman, Treasurer, and Secretary.

ARTICLE VI. MEETINGS

Section 1. Regular meetings of the Board shall be held every two weeks during the academic year, or as deemed necessary.

Section 2. Special meetings of the Board shall be held upon request of seven or more Board members or at the request of either the chairman or the faculty adviser of the organization involved.

ARTICLE VII. HONORARIA

Section 1. The Communications Board shall establish honoraria for the positions listed in Article III, Section 2, Bylaws.

Section 2. Such honoraria shall appear in the budget of the Student Communications Board in accordance with the amount specified in the bylaws of the Board.

ARTICLE VIII. CONSTITUTIONAL AMENDMENTS

Section 1. This constitution can be amended by a two-thirds vote of the total membership of the Board provided the proposed amendment shall have been:

A. Brought up for discussion at a prior meeting.

B. Submitted in writing to all members of the Student Communications Board.

C. Approved by the Student Senate, following approval by the Board.

BYLAWS

ARTICLE I. AMENDMENT OF THE BYLAWS

Section 1. These bylaws may be amended by a two-thirds vote of the Board provided that the amendment shall have been:

A. Brought up for discussion at a prior meeting.

B. Submitted in writing to all members of the Board.

C. Approved by Student Senate, following approval by the Board.

ARTICLE II. DUTIES

Section 1. The duties of the Student Communications Board shall be:

A. To receive a written monthly report from the executive officers of each member organization as to progress and developments, and further, to offer suggestions that will aid the efficient operations of these members.

B. To maintain written guides setting forth the requirements, responsibilities, and obligations of Board-appointed positions on the staffs of the various member organizations.

C. To set the deadlines for the receipt of petitions from candidates desiring appointment as executive officers of these organizations. Such appointments are to be made on such dates as determined by the Board and in accordance with the provisions as outlined in the body of this Constitution.

ARTICLE III. APPOINTMENT AND DISMISSAL OF EXECUTIVE OFFICERS

Section 1. Application for appointment

A. The Chairman of the Student Communications Board shall receive application petitions from all students who wish to apply for positions as executive officers.

B. The executive officers of each member organization are responsible for notifying staff members and the campus at large about upcoming vacancies in their positions, and about petitioning procedures.

C. The Student Communications Board is responsible for seeing that vacancies are well publicized.

Section 2. Petition procedures

A. The form of the petition for office must be approved by the Board during the winter quarter of each year.

B. Petitions shall normally be due the last official day of winter quarter, unless otherwise specified by the Board. Petitions will be available at least six weeks prior to the deadline.

C. Petition materials are confidential and will be sent to each voting member of the Board prior to the election meetings.

Section 3. Staff vote

A. The staff of the organization shall have three votes:

1. The staff vote (by secret ballot) shall be conducted at a meeting where candidates shall make presentations and answer questions from the staff.

2. Staff vote and the meetings with candidates shall be conducted by one of the Student Senate representatives on the Board and the Faculty adviser of the organization involved.

3. The current editorial (or managerial) and financial executives and members-at-large shall not participate in the staff vote and shall not be present at the staff meeting with the candidates.

4. The editorial (or managerial) and business executives and the representative-at-large shall draw up a list of regular staff members

for the staff vote. The list shall be posted
at least two weeks prior to the meeting with
candidates; anyone who is not included on
the staff list may register a complaint with
the faculty adviser or the Chairman of the
Board. Decision of the Board in such cases
shall be final.

5. The staff vote shall be split into three votes,
proportionate to the percentages of the total
that each candidate received.

6. The results of the staff vote shall be announced to the Board at the election meeting, prior to the balloting on candidates.
The staff vote shall remain confidential.

Section 4. The chairman of election meetings

A. Election meetings shall be conducted by the
Chairman of the Board. In the case of a tie
vote for a position, the chairman shall cast the
deciding vote; the treasurer of the Student
Communications Board shall cast the deciding
vote in an election in which the chairman is
involved. In the event that the chairman and
treasurer are involved, either as candidate or
voting member, the Board shall at a previous
meeting select another Board member who is
not involved to chair the election.

Section 5. The faculty adviser

A. The faculty adviser of each organization shall
be present at the election meetings as an ob-
server and resource person and may speak at
the request of the Board.

Section 6. Release of election results

A. The Chairman of the Board shall release the
selections for the executive officers immediately
after each election. The Board vote shall remain confidential.

ARTICLE IV. ELECTION OF OFFICERS

Section 1. The chairman, treasurer, and secretary shall be
elected from the student membership of the Board
by a majority vote of the Board. The vote shall be
taken at the first meeting of the new Board in the
Spring. Those eligible for offices and those voting
shall be members who will sit on the Board for
the following year. The outgoing chairman shall
cast the deciding vote in case of a tie.

ARTICLE V. DUTIES OF OFFICERS

Section 1. The chairman shall be the chief executive of the
Board and shall preside at meetings. He shall have

such additional powers as may be conferred and shall perform such other duties as prescribed by the Board.

Section 2. The treasurer shall keep an accurate account of all financial transactions of the Board and shall submit an annual budget to the Board of Budgets, after approval by the Student Communications Board. In the absence or inability of the chairman to perform his duties, the treasurer shall assume the duties of the chairman.

Section 3. The secretary shall maintain an active and complete file of the Board's actions and shall supply each Board member with minutes of the preceding meetings. One copy of the minutes is to be posted in the office of each organization.

ARTICLE VI. QUORUM

Section 1. A quorum for meetings membership shall be constituted by 50% plus one of the total of the Board, including at least one of the non-student members of the Board and a Student Senator.

ARTICLE VII. HONORARIA

Section 1. Honoraria may be changed by a two-thirds vote of the total membership of the Board. Advertising commissions may be changed by two-thirds vote of the Student Communications Board.

Section 2. Annual honoraria are to be as follows:

Cincinnatian Editor	$600.00
Cincinnatian Business Mgr.	325.00
News Record Editor	375.00
News Record Business Mgr.	375.00
Student Directory Editor	100.00
Student Directory Business Mgr.	66.00
Profile Editor	100.00
Profile Business Mgr.	66.00
WFIB General Mgr.	450.00
WFIB Sales Mgr.	450.00

Section 3. Payment of the honoraria shall be made as follows:

A. One-third of said honoraria to be paid at the end of the fall, winter, and spring quarters, except that honoraria for Profile will be paid entirely at the end of the year.

B. Approval of the Board:

1. The above honoraria shall be paid only upon the approval by the Student Communications Board.

2. The third payment shall be made only after the final audit of the books.

ARTICLE VIII. ADVERTISING COMMISSIONS
NEWS RECORD

Editor	$ 75.00/month
Business Mgr.	75.00/month
Advertising Mgr.	100.00/month plus 1% of national ads
Solicitors	25.00/month plus 6% of their customers' ads
Billing Clerk	50.00/month
Editorial Staff	200.00/month

(to be distributed at editor's discretion, subject to approval of the Board)

This is based on 9 month/year October through June, inclusive.

CINCINNATIAN

10% to Ad Solicitor
12% to the Editorial Staff
(to be distributed at editor's discretion, subject to approval of the Board)

PROFILE

15% to Ad Solicitor (for local ads only)

STUDENT DIRECTORY

14% to Ad Solicitor (for local ads only)

DRAUGHT

15% to Ad Solicitor (for local ads only)

WFIB

A. 5% of local advertising plus 5% of national advertising. This will be divided among the following management personnel: News Director, Program Director(s), Business Manager, Traffic Director, Continuity Director, Promotions, and one-half share to Sports Director. (Any of the above persons receiving academic credit for Radio Management lab will not receive a share.) Those shares will be divided among the remaining management personnel, subject to the approval of the Board and to be distributed at the General Manager's discretion. This is to be paid at the end of the fall, winter, and spring quarters.

B. Sales Manager. 5% of all local ads, to be paid at the end of the fall, winter, and spring quarters.

ARTICLE IX. STAFF MEMBERSHIP REQUIREMENTS

Section 1. The eligibility with respect to good standing of all candidates for publications offices shall be confirmed with the personnel deans by the faculty adviser of the organization involved.

ARTICLE X. REPORTS AND MANUALS OF PUBLICATIONS STAFFS

Section 1. Annual reports of Board-appointed members. All Board-appointed members of the publications staffs are to submit to their successors a report outlining the procedures followed during the previous year in carrying out the duties of their office and suggestions as to how these procedures may be improved.

Section 2. Finance Manuals

The business manager of each publication is to maintain a financial manual, outlining the financial procedures of his office.

Section 3. Third-quarter honoraria shall not be paid until the above requirements are met.

ARTICLES OF INCORPORATION FOR A COLLEGE SEPARATE PUBLISHING GROUP

PROPOSAL to the Board of Trustees of Ithaca (N.Y.) College, Agreement between Ithaca College and The Ithacan Publishing Company, and Certificate of Incorporation of The Ithacan Publishing Company.

PROPOSAL TO THE BOARD OF TRUSTEES

When a visitor comes to Ithaca College, the first thing he notices is the physical plant. This tells him something about the value that society places on education. The next thing he may see is a copy of the student newspaper. This reveals many of the values that the students place on their education.

The student newspaper is probably the best indication of the mood and temperament of a college's student body. It reflects not only their concerns, but their attitudes—Are they serious of purpose? Do they strive to do the best possible job? Do they set high, professional standards for themselves? etc.

It is in the best interests of both the students and the college to seek quality in the student newspaper.

The Ithacan has improved greatly since its first publication in 1935. It has grown with Ithaca College. It has reached the limits of achievement under present publishing conditions. It now would like to "move into the big leagues," and take the one step that can insure its continued growth—it would like to incorporate.

By incorporating, The Ithacan would emulate the widely

respected undergraduate publications of Cornell, Harvard, Yale, Princeton, Columbia, Brown, UCLA, the University of Wisconsin, the University of Illinois, Boston University, and the University of Michigan.

In every one of these cases, it has been found that incorporation of the student newspaper has been advantageous to both the newspaper and the university.

The newspaper, by incorporating, would take upon itself greater responsibility. As an independent corporation, the editors and the Board of Directors would be accountable for everything in the paper. The paper would operate under the conditions similar to those of the outside world, which would enable the staff to acquire valuable experience for vocations, in writing, printing, editing and advertising. Under a Board of Directors chosen for its experience, this would be superior training in these fields.

The newspaper would have to meet greater standards of professionalism set by professionals.

By incorporating, The Ithacan would be able to move toward the use of newer and more modern printing methods and, hopefully, lower its printing costs. This would allow for greater, expanded coverage of campus news events.

The incorporation of The Ithacan would also prove advantageous to the college. The college's Business Office would immediately be relieved of the considerable time, effort, and expense now involved in handling The Ithacan accounts.

The college would no longer be directly responsible for The Ithacan, either for libel suits or community complaints.

It is hoped that by incorporating, The Ithacan would eventually become financially self-sufficient, thereby saving the college the $40,000 with which it presently subsidizes the paper.

The specifics of financial independence are listed below:

A. The Ithacan Corporation will be run by a Board of Directors, composed of respected members of the academic and business community of Ithaca and vicinity.

B. The Ithacan Corporation will agree to sell to the college copies of The Ithacan, in an agreed-upon size and quantity, each year. The Ithacan will agree to sell Ithaca College 4,000 copies of the newspaper weekly (during the academic year) for a price to be agreed upon in the near future.

C. The Board of Directors, upon the recommendation of The Ithacan staff, shall appoint the President of the Corporation (Editor-in-Chief) and Treasurer of the Corporation (Business Manager) who shall be responsible for the day-to-day functioning of the paper.

D. The Editor-in-Chief shall appoint all members of the editorial board subject to the approval of the staff and the Board of Directors.

E. Under present conditions it is estimated that The Ithacan would average 14 pages per issue, a minimum of 25 issues a year, and 4,000 copies per issue.

F. The Ithacan will be published in the interest of the entire college community—the students, the faculty and the administration.

G. The Board of Directors, in conjunction with the Editorial Board, shall determine what salaries or scholarships persons working for the corporation will receive.

H. The college would charge the Ithacan Corporation nominal fees for the rental of space and the acquisition of equipment presently being used by The Ithacan.

I. The initial Board of Directors would be appointed by a committee composed of the Editor, Business Manager, Managing Editor, Dean of Students, the College Vice President of Business and Finance, Director of Public Affairs, and an ex-officio member from the Student Government.

AGREEMENT

THIS AGREEMENT, made this 28th day of July, 1969, by and between ITHACA COLLEGE, a New York State Educational Corporation of Danby Road, Ithaca, Tompkins County, New York, hereinafter referred to as "College," and THE ITHACAN PUBLISHING COMPANY, an unincorporated association and its successors, having a principal office and place of business on Danby Road, Ithaca, Tompkins County, New York, hereinafter referred to as "The Ithacan," witnesseth:

WHEREAS, the College has heretofore published a student newspaper, entitled "The Ithacan," and

WHEREAS, the Editorial Board of The Ithacan has expressed the desire of forming a corporation and having the corporation, as a separate and distinct entity from Ithaca College, publish a student newspaper, and engage in related publishing activities, and

WHEREAS, the Board of Trustees of Ithaca College has heretofore approved the severance of the student newspaper from the control and jurisdiction of the College and has approved the granting of the sole right to publish and distribute a student newspaper called The Ithacan, and

WHEREAS, The Ithacan has agreed to publish and distribute a student newspaper at Ithaca College and has agreed to be solely and entirely responsible for its editorial content, and the contents of other related publications, and for the publication and delivery thereof.

NOW, THEREFORE, in consideration of the premises and the mutual provisos herein contained, it is agreed as follows:

1. The College agrees to and does hereby furnish The Ithacan the exclusive use of Room 104 (Darkroom) and Room 103 (Office) in the West Tower on the Ithaca College campus, and agrees to provide heat, light and necessary maintenance for said premises for $250 per year.

2. The College agrees to and hereby does sell to The Ithacan the personal property and equipment set forth in the inventory hereto annexed, heretofore used by the College in the

publication of a student newspaper, for the sum of $1,000. Said sum shall be amortized over a five-year period by the payment of $200 per annum on the first day of January each year, commencing January 1, 1970, without interest.

3. The College agrees to and does hereby subscribe to a number of newspapers of each issue that equals 70 percent of the then current student body as determined by the Registrar's Office of the College.

4. The Ithacan agrees to furnish to the College on dates to be determined by The Ithacan, the number of newspapers as required by paragraph 3 of this agreement and further agrees to deliver these newspapers in such quantities and to such locations on the Campus that the administration of the College may designate. It is the intention of The Ithacan to publish 23 or 24 issues (the present schedule of issues) during the regular academic year —excluding summer sessions: a summer edition is not covered by this agreement.

5. The College agrees to pay for its subscription as above set forth, the following amounts:

For the first year of operations $20,050
For the second year of operations $18,550
For the third year of operations $17,050
For the fourth year of operations and for
    each year thereafter or until renegotiated
    with the approval of both parties $14,050

6. It is agreed that the College will pay to The Ithacan on or about the 1st day of September, 1969, the sum of $10,025, representing one-half of the above payment for the first year of operations, it being understood and agreed, however, that the College may deduct from said payment any monies advanced to The Ithacan for legal fees or other expenses related to its incorporation.

7. It is understood and agreed that after the first year, the College will pay The Ithacan for its subscription for newspapers as above specified on a monthly basis at the rate of one-ninth of the annual commitment, said payment to be made on the first of each month of the academic year, September through May.

8. The College agrees to and does hereby sell, transfer and assign to The Ithacan the exclusive rights to publish a student newspaper on the Ithaca College campus, to solicit advertisements and subscriptions for this newspaper to engage in all activities reasonably connected with the publication of a student newspaper, and to use the name and title of "The Ithacan."

9. The parties agree that the authority to select editorial policies and content of the newspaper shall be vested exclusively with the Editorial Board of The Ithacan and that The Ithacan shall be solely responsible therefor.

10. In view of the fact that the College has committed itself to the payment of considerable sums for subscriptions to newspapers and also in view of the fact that The Ithacan is indebted to the College as above set forth for an indebtedness covering

a period of five years, The Ithacan agrees to furnish to the College an annual audit of its books. Such audit shall be submitted to the Treasurer of the College in sufficient detail to enable him to make reasonable judgment as to the financial condition of The Ithacan.

In this connection, however, it is understood and agreed that this audit may be accomplished by students in the Economics and Business Administration Department of Ithaca College who are not affiliated in any manner with The Ithacan, provided that the audit is conducted under the guidance and supervision of a Professor of Accounting, and that the audit bears his signature.

11. The Ithacan shall make advertising space available at its discretion to selected offices and agencies of the College at a rate per column inch of printing cost plus 10 percent.

12. It is expressly understood and agreed that The Ithacan is presently in the process of incorporating under the statute of the State of New York, and that all rights and obligations of The Ithacan pursuant to this agreement shall inure to the benefit of and be assumed by the corporate successor of The Ithacan.

13. The Ithacan will purchase an adequate amount of liability insurance which protects the College as well as the interests of The Ithacan. The College shall be furnished with a certificate of insurance indicating the existence of this protection.

14. This contract can be cancelled by either party at any time by giving to the other sixty days written notice to cancel. Such letter to be presented to the President of each institution.

ITHACA COLLEGE
By: *Howard Dillingham*
As: *President*
By: *Richard A. Cohen*
As: *Business Manager*

CERTIFICATE OF INCORPORATION

Certificate of Incorporation of The Ithacan Publishing Company, Inc., pursuant to the Membership Corporations Law.

1. The Name of the proposed corporation shall be The Ithacan Publishing Company, Inc.

2. The purposes for which the corporation is to be formed are: to publish, print and sell a student newspaper, daily, weekly, or monthly, for the edification and entertainment of students, faculty and alumni of Ithaca College; to gather news, solicit advertisements and subscriptions; to do general printing of all kinds, including the printing of brochures, announcements and publications for Ithaca College; and generally to do all things that those engaged in a similar publishing activity customarily do.

3. In pursuance of and not in limitation of the general powers conferred by law, and the purposes hereinabove set forth, it is expressly provided that this corporation shall have the power to do all such acts as are necessary or convenient to attain the objects and purposes herein set forth, to the same extent and

as fully as any natural person could or might do, and as are not forbidden by law or by this certificate of incorporation, or by the bylaws of this corporation.

It is further expressly provided that this corporation, as a non-profit corporation, shall have the power to purchase, lease, hold, sell, mortgage, receive by gift, device or bequest, or otherwise acquire or dispose of such real or personal property as may be necessary to the purposes of this corporation.

4. The territory in which the operation of the corporation will be principally conducted is Tompkins County, New York.

5. The principal office of the corporation is to be located on the Ithaca College campus, in the Town of Ithaca, County of Tompkins and State of New York.

6. The number of its directors shall be three.

7. The names and residences of its directors, until the first annual meeting, are as follows:

Richard A. Cohen, 509 Lake Street, Ithaca, New York;

Mrs. Alison D. Cohen, 509 Lake Street, Ithaca, New York;

Michael Hinkelman, 110 Salem Drive, Ithaca, New York.

8. All the subscribers hereto are of full age; all of them are citizens of the United States; at least one of them is a resident of the State of New York; and that of the persons named as directors, all are citizens of the United States and at least one is a resident of the State of New York.

9. The corporation is not organized for pecuniary profit; it shall have no stock or stockholders and none of the income or surplus assets of the corporation, if any, shall be distributed in dividends to members or for the personal profit of any individual or non-charitable or non-educational institution or corporation.

IN WITNESS WHEREOF we have made, signed, acknowledged and filed this certificate in duplicate.

Dated this 11th day of July, 1969.

Richard A. Cohen

Alison D. Cohen

Michael Hinkelman

Edward F. Arnold

APPENDIX G

CAMPUS BROADCAST STATION POLICY STATEMENT

FROM Melvyn M. Muchnik, "The State Is Not Necessarily The Unfettered Master Of All It Creates," *Journal of College Radio*, November 1971. Excerpts from the report of the Ad Hoc Committee on the University of Denver FM Station, a student-faculty committee created to make recommendations concerning the radio station's role and policy, management and budget.

THE ROLE OF THE STATION

Classically, commercial radio stations define their functions and responsibilities in the somewhat amorphous categories of information, education and entertainment. These categories, normally described in a station's license application to the Federal Communications Commission, are in practice translated to programming that the station hopes will garner the largest possible audience. For the commercial station, large audiences mean advertising dollars. Such commercial considerations run counter to broad altruistic objectives allowing a station to serve but a few of the myriad needs of the community it serves.

Ideally, broadcasting should cater to as wide a variety of tastes as possible, the tastes of small audiences and of mass audiences, of cultural minorities and cultural majorities. Ours is a pluralistic society, in culture as well as in ethnic origins and styles of life of its people. A medium of expression as pervasive as radio should reflect and enrich this cultural pluralism. It is in this context that the Committee sees the potential and opportunity offered by non-commercial public radio.

By terms of its license, the University of Denver FM station, KCFR, has agreed to serve the "public interest, convenience, and necessity." It has responsibilities both to the University community and to the larger Denver community. Because of the delicate relationship between the licensee, the Board of Trustees, and the student funding agency, the station cannot be, nor does the Committee feel it should be, an "official" voice of the University of Denver. The station is to be a primarily student operated activity and as such does not reflect any "official" position of the University of Denver. Rather, it can reflect the diverse tastes and expression represented within the University community.

The Committee believes that the station's primary audience should be the University of Denver community, particularly its student community. It is this community that should readily yield an audience desirous of being exposed to inquiry, exploration, innovation and experimentation. Further, it is our belief that within the larger Denver community, there exist many individuals with similar desires. This larger community wants to know what is new in literature, drama, the sciences, music, public affairs and news. It superimposes such groups as educators, students and the youthful community of Denver. We do not believe that such a posture necessarily defines the station as serving an elitist audience.

Because of its non-commercial nature, the burden of our responsibility is greater in presenting areas of social concern because we cannot allow a singular point of view to dominate. We must seek out as many viewpoints as feasible. In pursuing these goals, controversy may arise, but at least it reaches across the gap of misunderstanding and even the most irreconcilable opposition can begin to gain insight into opposing points of view. The position of this station is exploratory rather than inflammatory. The philosophy of freedom and education can best be reached by combining the resources of both the University and the larger Denver community. There is more to the University of Denver than Denver, Colorado, and there is more to Denver, Colorado, than the University of Denver. We must use all the available resources at our disposal if we are to serve the "public interest, convenience, and necessity."

Both of these communities have limited resources and to stay within the confines of any one of these communities is, in fact, restricting our purpose as a public radio station. The Denver community has to serve as a complement to the University resources as a source of program material. Involvement between the University and the community does not mean that the University is taking a stand as an institution but rather, that it is using its resources to help make the community aware of its problems. Conversely, the community should be able to achieve the same interaction with the University. In serving such a valuable function, the University of Denver will be making a necessary and worthwhile contribution to the Denver community while not jeopardizing its position as an institution for intellectual pursuit. Ideally, we will try to tap all available sources, be it local, national, or worldwide.

STATEMENT OF KCFR STATION POLICY

KCFR exists to engage in broadcasting under terms of a license granted by the Federal Communications Commission. The Radio Board is the representative of the licensee in the formation and review of policy pertaining to both programming and station management. While it is not intended that the Board dictate program policy on a day-to-day basis, the Board does have responsibility to insure that KCFR stays within the policy set forth by the Board and all applicable rules and regulations.

The General Manager as the chief administrative officer of KCFR executes the responsibility of the Board in the day-to-day operation of the station and with respect to all programs broadcast by KCFR. The General Manager, the student Program Director, and staff of KCFR have the responsibility to conduct themselves in accord with the highest standards of broadcasting ethics and will subscribe to the program standards set forth on the Radio Code of the National Association of Broadcasters.

The student Program Director as the selectee of the Radio Board is vested with the day-to-day program operations of the station including the development of working schedules and staff relationships.

The General Manager and Program Director may delegate to program producers and other staff personnel that degree of authority and responsibility required to enable them to accomplish their tasks. No delegation, however, relieves the Program Director of his responsibility to the General Manager, or the General Manager of his responsibility to the Radio Board for every broadcast that is made on the station.

KCFR program policies specified by the Radio Board shall from time to time be reviewed. The Radio Board shall maintain the broadest possible program policies concerning what types of programs shall be aired to serve the station's audiences in the most relevant and responsible manner possible. It shall be the responsibility of the General Manager to execute those policies. Any willful violation of KCFR program policies by KCFR staff personnel shall be grounds for dismissal from the staff.

Nothing in the stated policies of KCFR is intended to conflict with the provisions of the Communications Act of 1934 as amended, the Rules and Regulations of the Federal Communications Commission, or the broadcast provisions of the U.S. Criminal Code. The latter documents shall in all cases prevail.

As a matter of general policy, the KCFR General Manager and other top echelon programming and engineering personnel shall be thoroughly familiar with Subpart C of Volume III of the Rules and Regulations of the Federal Communications Commission pertaining to non-commercial FM broadcast stations. Internal procedures shall be developed by the staff of KCFR to insure strict adherence to applicable provisions of Subpart C by all appropriate station personnel. Particular notation shall be made of engineering and logging requirements.

PROGRAM POLICIES

1. KCFR may not advocate breaking the law.
2. KCFR shall strictly comply with provisions of the U.S. Criminal Code prohibiting broadcast of obscene, profane and indecent language as well as information concerning lotteries, and broadcast involving fraud. While it is recognized that determination of material as either profane or obscene is often difficult, the standards to be applied extend beyond the University community to the Denver community. In all cases, the on-air personnel of KCFR shall exercise reason and good taste in recognizing its responsibility to the broader based community.
3. It is a law of the United States that profane, obscene and indecent language uttered in a radio broadcast shall subject the persons who utter or permit utterance of to a fine of $10,000 and prison sentence of not more than two years. The General Manager is responsible for informing station personnel and program particpants of this law, especially in preparation for live programs. (18USC464)
4. Whenever a word or phrase regarded in ordinary usage as profane, indecent or obscene appears in any broadcast tape or script, the program producer shall refrain from broadcasting the program without the specific authority of the General Manager. The General Manager may decide, on his authority, that, although usually regarded as indecent, obscene or profane, a word or phrase is either,
   a). necessary for the artistic integrity of a work of literary art, and can on those grounds be defended; or

b). so intimate a part of a situation being dealt with by a public affairs program that the character of the situation would be grossly misrepresented by omitting the word or phrase. Whenever under such circumstances the General Manager exercises this authority, he shall notify the Radio Advisory Board in writing that he has done so, and if possible, such notification shall be given before the program is broadcast.

5. Whenever the presentation of any subject matter involves presentation or discussion of attitudes or actions that violate general standards of respectability, especially in regard to sexual behavior or morals, the program producer shall call the subject matter to the attention of the General Manager. The General Manager shall be responsible for determining the time at which the matter shall be broadcast, if in his judgment special care in handling the matter is warranted. If the General Manager determines that the matter is likely to violate community standards to an extent that could result in punitive action by the FCC or other legal action, he shall refer the decision about whether to broadcast the program to the Radio Board.

6. It shall be the general policy of KCFR to avoid provoking community attitudes, with respect to profanity, obscenity, or sexual behavior or morals. If provocation is deemed unavoidable and is in the interest of broadening the perspectives, reshaping perceptions or opening new possibilities to the radio audience, then the broadcast shall be conducted in a manner that is serious, articulate, respectful of law and community making processes, and shall base its claim to be heard against the community standards on the persuasiveness of the facts or reasons it offers, or the authority of the participants in their fields of work.

7. While KCFR is not required by law to permit use of its facilities by any legally qualified candidates for public office, permission extended to one candidate requires that all other candidates for that office be afforded equal opportunity to use the station's facilities. It is noted that the law prohibits any power of censorship over the material broadcast by any such candidate.

8. By law, KCFR is responsible for all material broadcast over its facilities whether originated locally or received through network or other outside sources. Procedures shall be developed by the staff of KCFR to insure adequate review of all material received from outside sources prior to broadcast with the exception that the station may not exercise censorship over material broadcast by legally qualified candidates as indicated in the previous section.

9. The Fairness Doctrine of the Federal Communications Commission provides that where a licensee affords time for an opinion on a controversial issue of public importance it is under an obligation to afford reasonable opportunities for

the presentation of conflicting views. In fulfilling this obligation, KCFR shall actively seek opposing views to matters broadcast which are determined to be both controversial and of public importance.

10. KCFR shall strictly comply with Section 399 of the Public Broadcasting Act of 1967 which precludes editorialization or support or opposition of any candidate for public office by noncommercial educational broadcasting sections.

11. All appeals concerning the radio station will be handled by the Radio Board. An appeal of the Radio Board's decisions may be made to the Vice Chancellor for Student Affairs.

12. The General Manager is expected to bring before the Radio Board critical matters concerning station policy.

APPENDIX H

EXCERPTS FROM FEDERAL COMMUNICATIONS COMMISSION RULES AND REGULATIONS FOR EDUCATIONAL BROADCAST STATIONS

FROM *Rules and Regulations of the Federal Communications Commission, Part 73, Radio Broadcast Services* (Washington, D.C.: Government Printing Office, 1968 and subsequent amendments).

EXCERPTS FROM SUBPART C—NONCOMMERCIAL EDUCATIONAL FM BROADCAST STATIONS

In considering the assignment of a channel for a noncommercial educational FM broadcast station, the Commission will take into consideration the extent to which each application meets the requirements of any statewide plan for noncommercial educational FM broadcast stations filed with the Commission, provided that such plans afford fair treatment to public and private educational institutions, urban and rural, at the primary, secondary, higher, and adult educational levels, and appear otherwise fair and equitable.

The operation of, and the service furnished by noncommercial educational FM broadcast stations shall be governed by the following:

(a) A noncommercial educational FM broadcast station will be licensed only to a nonprofit educational organization and upon showing that the station will be used for the advancement of an educational program.

(1) In determining the eligibility of publicly supported educational organizations, the accreditation of their respective state departments of education shall be taken into consideration.

(2) In determining the eligibility of privately controlled educational organizations, the accreditation of state departments of education and/or recognized regional and national educational accrediting organizations shall be taken into consideration.

(b) Each station may transmit programs directed to specific schools in a system or systems for use in connection with the regular courses as well as routine and administrative material pertaining thereto and may transmit educational, cultural, and entertainment programs to the public.

(c) A noncommercial educational FM broadcast station may broadcast programs produced by, or at the expense of, or furnished by persons other than the licensee, if no other consideration than the furnishing of the program and the costs incidental to its production and broadcast are received by the licensee. The payment of line charges by another station, network, or someone other than the licensee of a noncommercial educational FM broadcast station, or general contributions to the operating costs of a station, shall not be considered as being prohibited by this paragraph.

(d) Each station shall furnish a nonprofit and noncommercial broadcast service. . . . No announcements promoting the sale of a product or service shall be broadcast in connection with any program.

Noncommercial educational stations . . . are divided into four classes, as follows:

(1) A Class D educational station is one operating with no more than 10 watts transmitter power output. Class D stations may be assigned in all zones, on any of the channels specified in 73.501.

(2) Noncommercial educational stations with more than 10 watts transmitter output are classified as Class A, Class B, or Class C depending on the effective radiated power and antenna height above average terrain, and the zone in which the station's transmitter is located. . . .

See Subpart D of Part 1 (of the FCC rules and regulations) for general requirements as to applications, filing of applications and description of application forms, other forms and information to be filed with the Commission, the manner in which applications are processed, and provisions applying to action on applications. See 1.1111 of Subpart G of that part for the fees to be paid in connection with applications for facilities in the service covered in this subpart.

Initial licenses for noncommercial educational FM stations will ordinarily be issued for a period running until the date specified in this section for the State or territory in which the station is located or, if issued after such date, to the next triennial renewal date determined in accordance with this section; and, when renewed, will normally be renewed for 3 years: Provided, however, That, if the Commission finds that the public interest, convenience or necessity will be served thereby, it may issue either an initial license or a renewal thereof for a lesser term.

Noncommercial educational FM broadcast stations are not required to operate on a regular schedule and no minimum number of hours of operation is specified; but the hours of actual operation during a license period shall be taken into consideration in considering the renewal of noncommercial educational FM broadcast licenses wherever it appears that the channels available for such stations are insufficient to meet the demand.

The licensee of each station shall notify the Commission in Washington, D.C., and the Engineer in Charge of the radio district in which the station is located of permanent discontinuance of operation at least two days before operation is discontinued. The licensee shall, in addition, immediately forward the station license and other instruments of authorization to the Washington, D.C., office of the Commission for cancellation.

A "legally qualified candidate" means any person who has publicly announced that he is a candidate for nomination by a convention of a political party or for nomination or election in a primary, special, or general election, municipal, county, state or national, and who meets the qualifications prescribed by the applicable laws to hold the office for which he is a candidate, so that he may be voted for by the electorate directly or by means of delegates or electors, and who—

(1) Has qualified for a place on the ballot or

(2) Is eligible under the applicable law to be voted for by sticker, by writing in his name on the ballot, or other method and (i) has been duly nominated by a political party which is commonly known and regarded as such, or (ii) makes a substantial showing that he is a bona fide candidate for nomination or office, as the case may be.

General Requirements. No station licensee is required to permit the use of its facilities by any legally qualified candidate for public office, but if any licensee shall permit any such candidate to use its facilities, it shall afford equal opportunities to all other such candidates for that office to use such facilities: Provided, That such licensee shall have no power of censorship over the material broadcast by any such candidate.

Practices. No licensee shall make any discrimination in practices, regulations, facilities, or services for or in connection with the service rendered pursuant to this part, or make or give any preference to any candidate for public office or subject any such candidate to any prejudice or disadvantage; nor shall any licensee make any contract or other agreement which shall have the effect of permitting any legally qualified candidate for any public office to broadcast to the exclusion of other legally qualified candidates for the same public office.

Records; inspection. Every licensee shall keep and permit public inspection of a complete record of all requests for broadcast time made by or on behalf of candidates for public office, together with an appropriate notation showing the disposition made by the licensee of such requests. Such records shall be retained for a period of two years.

Time of request. A request for equal opportunities must be submitted to the licensee within 1 week of the day on which the first prior use, giving rise to the right to equal opportunities, occurred: Provided, however, That where a person was not a candidate at the time of such first prior use, he shall submit his request within 1 week of the first subsequent use after he has become a legally qualified candidate for the office in question.

Burden of proof. A candidate requesting such equal opportunities of the licensee, or complaining of non-compliance to the Commission shall have the burden of proving that he and his opponent are legally qualified candidates for the same public office.

When, during the presentation of views on a controversial issue of public importance, an attack is made upon the honesty, character, integrity or like personal qualities of an identified person or group, the licensee shall, within a reasonable time and in no event later than 1 week after the attack, transmit to the person or group attacked (1) notification of the date, time and identification of the broadcast; (2) a script or tape (or an accurate summary if a script or tape is not available) of the attack; and (3) an offer of a reasonable opportunity to respond over the licensee's facilities.

APPENDIX I

DISTRIBUTION GUIDELINES FOR HIGH SCHOOL PUBLICATIONS

FROM the National Association of Secondary School Principals' *Legal Memorandum,* October 1971. The following guidelines were upheld in *Goodman* v. *Board of Education* (New Jersey Commissioner's Decision, March 12, 1971).

A. *Places:* On the school sidewalk in front of the main entrance to building and the walk in front of the gym lobby. (In case of bad weather, two pupils only would be permitted each in the front main lobby and in the gym lobby. Specific approval to distribute materials inside would be required each time.)

B. *Time:* 7:45–8:15 a.m., 2:46–3:15 p.m.

C. *Approval:* The previous day or earlier by appropriate class dean or principal, if dean should be absent. For materials not readily classifiable or approvable, more than one day should be allowed.

D. *Littering:* All distributed items which are dropped in the immediate area (on the front sidewalk and lawn to the street, for example, or the two inside lobbies and adjacent corridor for 50–75 feet) must be removed by persons distributing material. Wastebaskets will be provided.

E. *Unacceptable items:* So-called "hate" literature which scurrilously attacks ethnic, religious and racial groups, other irresponsible publications aimed at creating hostility and violence, hardcore pornography, and similar materials are not suitable for distribution in the school.

Materials denigrating to specific individuals in or out of the school.

Materials designed for commercial purposes—to advertise a product or service for sale or rent.

Materials which are designed to solicit funds, unless approved by the Superintendent or his assistant.

Literature which in any manner and in any part thereof promotes, favors or opposes the candidacy of any candidate for election at any annual school election, or the adoption of any bond issue, proposal, or any public question submitted at any general, municipal or school election.

F. *Acceptable materials:* Materials not proscribed in section E unless dean or principal should be convinced that the item would materially disrupt classwork or involve substantial disorder or invasion of the rights of others.

G. *Appeal:* Pupil approval may appeal to the principal who with a student advisory committee of one representative from each class will review the matter. Should the petition be denied, the petitioner may still appeal to the Superintendent, then to the Board of Education.

APPENDIX J

Excerpts from Post Office
Second-Class Mailing Permit Regulations

From "Mailing Permits," "How to Prepare Second- and Third-Class Mailings," Chapter I, *Postal Service Manual.*

125.5 Statement and Copy Filed with Mailings
.51 Copies Filed by Publishers
.511 Copy To Show Compliance with Basic Second-Class Requirements

The publisher must file a copy of each issue with the postmaster at the original entry office.

.512 Copy Marked To Show Advertising

The publisher must file, either with the postmaster of the original entry office or the postmaster of the additional entry office where the publication is produced or prepared for mailing, a copy of each edition of each issue marked by the publisher in such a manner that the advertisements in the copy may be verified when necessary.

.54 Endorsements on Marked Copy And Form 3542

The total advertising and nonadvertising portions must be determined by column inches, square inches, pages, or by any other recognized units of measure. The publisher must show by endorsement on the first page of the copy the total units of the advertising space and the total units of nonadvertising space and the percentage of each.

.55 Verification Of Advertising Percentage

The postmaster must verify the advertising percentage reported on Form 3542 by actual measurement of the advertising and nonadvertising portions of one issue at least once a year. If discrepancies are noted, more frequent verification must be made to establish the accuracy of the publisher's figures. A record of the verification will be made on the reverse of the applicable Form 3542 or the papers attached thereto.

.56 Payment of Advertising Rates on Reading Portions

A publisher may, if he so desires, pay postage at the advertising zone rates on both the advertising and nonadvertising portions instead of marking a copy of each issue to show the advertising and nonadvertising portions. When the advertising exceeds 75 percent, the copies filed must have endorsed on the first page by the publisher the words "Advertising over 75 percent." When the advertising does not exceed 75 percent, the copies must have endorsed on the first page by the publisher the words "Advertising not over 75 percent."

132.2 Qualifications For Second-Class Privileges

.21 What May Qualify

.211 Mailable Publications

Only newspapers and other periodical publications which meet the mailability criteria established in Part 124 may be mailed at the second-class rates.

.212 With Or Without General Advertising

All publications that meet the basic qualifications explained in 132.22 may carry general advertising. The publications of the institutions and societies specifically named in 132.23 must meet all the basic qualifications except the requirement of a paid subscription list. They are excused from having a paid list only when they do not carry general advertising. Those that carry general advertising must have a paid list.

.22 Basic Qualifications

.221 Regular Issuance

Publishers must determine the number of issues they will

publish each year and adopt a statement of frequency that will show at what regular intervals the issues will appear. Examples of statements of frequency are:

Daily	Semiweekly
Weekly	Biweekly
Monthly	Semimonthly
Quarterly	Weekly during school year
Monthly except during July	Four times a year in
and August	January, February,
	October and November

A publication may not be published under a frequency that provides for less than four issues each year. Issues must be published regularly as called for by the statement of frequency. Publishers may change the number of issues scheduled and adopt a new statement of frequency by filing an application for second-class reentry. (See 132.34.) . . .

.222 Issuance at Known Office

Publications must be issued and mailed at a known office of publication. A known office of publication is a public office where the business of the publication is transacted during the usual business hours. The office must be maintained at the place where the publication has been granted original second-class mail privileges. Offices for the transaction of business may be maintained at more than one place, but mailings may be accepted at the second-class pound rates only at the post offices where regional or additional mail privileges have been authorized.

.223 Preparation

Publications must be formed of printed sheets. They may not be reproduced by stencil, mimeograph, or hectograph processes or reproduced in imitation of typewriting. Reproduction by stencil, mimeograph, or hectograph processes is reproduction in imitation of typewriting and is not permissible. Reproduction by any other printing process is permissible. Any style of type may be used.

.224 Contents

Publications must be originated and published for the purpose of disseminating information of a public character, or they must be devoted to literature, the sciences, art, or some special industry.

.225 List of Subscribers

Publications must have a legitimate list of persons who have subscribed by paying or promising to pay at a rate above nominal . . . for copies to be received during a stated time.

.23 Publications of Institutions and Societies

.231 Publications that do not have subscribers and that are issued as follows may contain only the publishers' own advertising and not under any conditions the advertising of other persons, institutions, or concerns:

By a regularly incorporated institution of learning, by a regularly established State institution of learning supported

in whole or in part by public taxation, including bulle-
tins issued by State boards of health, State industrial development agencies, State conservation and fish and
game agencies or departments, and State boards or departments of public charities and corrections, and by a
public or nonprofit private elementary or secondary institution of learning or its administrative or governing
body and program announcements or guides published
by an educational radio or television agency of a State
or political subdivision thereof or by a nonprofit educational radio or television station.

.232 Publications that do not have subscribers and that are
issued as follows may contain only the publishers' own advertising:

By or under the auspices of a benevolent or fraternal society
or order organized under the lodge system and having
an actual membership of not less than 1,000 persons or
of a trades-union; or as the publications of strictly professional, literary, historical, or scientific societies; or
by churches and church organizations.

.25 Identification Statements In Copies

Copies of publications must be identified as second-class mail
by having the following items printed on one of the first five
pages in a position where they may be easily located by postal
employees and other interested persons:

a. Name of publication. The name of the publication must be
shown on the front in a position and in a style and size of
type that will make it clearly distinguishable from the name
of the publisher or other items on the front.

b. Date of issue.

c. Statement of frequency

d. Issue number. The copies of each issue must be numbered
consecutively. The consecutive numbering of published issues may not be broken by assigning numbers to issues un-
avoidably omitted.

e. Subscription price, if the publication has one.

f. Name of known office of publication and ZIP Code, including
street and number when there is letter-carrier service, must
be printed in a position or in a style and size of type or with
a designation that will make it clearly distinguishable from
the names of other offices of the publication. When there is
no post office at the place where published, the name of the
post office where mailed must be shown as the office of publication. Addresses in mastheads and datelines must be printed
so they will clearly show where change of address notices, un-
deliverable copies, orders for subscriptions, and other mail
items are to be sent. See 125.26.

g. Second-class imprint, reading Second-class postage paid at
_____. When a publication is mailed at two or more
offices, the imprint must read Second-class postage paid at
_____ and at additional mailing offices.

h. Notice of pending application, when copies are mailed while an application is pending, reading Application to mail at second-class postage rates is pending at _____.

132.3 Applications For Second-Class Privileges

.31 Applications for Publications and News Agents That Do Not Have Second-Class Privileges

An application must be filed by the publisher before a publication may be mailed at the second-class rates. Two copies of the issue described in the application must also be filed. When one-half or more of the total copies distributed are purchased by news agents for resale or are consigned to news agents for sale, two copies each of at least four issues must be filed before an application is either approved or disapproved, to demonstrate compliance with the requirement for regular issuance at least four times each year. . . .

Copies of all application forms may be obtained from local postmasters. The headings on the forms describe what information must be furnished by publishers and news agents. Use the following forms:

a. File application Form 3501 for second-class mail privileges for a publication that meets the basic qualifications (see 132.22) at the post office of the place where the known office of publication is located. . . .

b. File application Form 3502 for second-class mail privileges for a publication of an institution or society (see 132.23) that does not meet the basic qualifications at the post office of the place where the known office of publication is located. . . .

.32 Acceptance After Application Is Filed

Publishers or news agents may not mail at the second-class rates until the application for second-class privileges is approved by the Director, Office of Mail Classification, Bureau of Finance and Administration. See 132.36. Postmasters may not accept mailings at the second-class rates until they receive a written authorization from the Director, Office of Mail Classification. Postage at the applicable third- or fourth-class rates may be paid in money on mailings made while an application is pending. The postmaster will keep a record of such mailings on Form 3503, Record of Deposits Made While Second-Class Application Is Pending, and if second-class privileges are authorized by the Director, Office of Mail Classification, he will be instructed to return to the publishers or news agents the difference between the third- or fourth-class rates and the second-class rates. Form 3503 will not be kept and the difference will not be returned when postage is paid by stamps affixed.

.34 Reentry Because Of Change In Name, Frequency, or Location

When the name or frequency is changed, an application for reentry must be filed on Form 3510 at the post office of original entry, accompanied by two copies of the publication showing the new name or frequency. . . .

.35 Fees

The fees to accompany applications for second-class original entry, reentry, or additional entry, or for registration as a news agent, are:

Kind	Amount
Original entry—circulation not more than 2,000	$30
Original entry—circulation 2,001 to 5,000	60
Original entry—circulation 5,001 and over	120

If an application is not approved, no part of the fee is returned to the applicant.

.36 Granting Or Denial Of Application

The Director, Office of Mail Classification, Bureau of Finance and Administration, rules on all applications. If he grants the application, he notifies the postmaster at the office where the application for original entry was filed, who in turn notifies the applicant. Before taking action on an application, the Director may call on the publisher for additional information or evidence to support or clarify the application. Failure of the publisher to furnish the information requested may be cause for denial of the application as incomplete or, on its face, not fulfilling the requirements for entry. If the Director denies the application, he must notify the publisher specifying the reasons for the denial. The denial becomes effective in 15 days from receipt of the notice by the publisher unless the publisher appeals therefrom.

132.6 Ownership, Management and Circulation Statement

.61 Requirements, as Contained in 39 U.S. Code, 4369.

.611 Each owner of a publication having second-class mail privileges under 39 U.S. Code, 4354 (see 132.22) shall furnish to the Postmaster General at least once a year, and shall publish in such publication once a year, information in such form and detail and at such time as he may require respecting—

a. The identity of the editor, managing editor, publishers, and owners;
b. The identity of the corporation and stockholders thereof, if the publication is owned by a corporation;
c. The identity of known bondholders, mortgagees, and other security holders;
d. The extent and nature of the circulation of the publication, including, but not limited to, the number of copies distributed, the methods of distribution, and the extent to which such circulation is paid in whole or in part; and
e. Such other information as he may deem necessary to determine whether the publication meets the standards for second-class mail privileges.

The Postmaster General shall not require the names of persons owning less than 1 per centum of the total amount of stocks, bonds, mortgages, or other securities.

.622 Publishers who file a statement under the provisions of section 132.611 shall publish the complete statement in the second issue thereafter of the publication to which it relates. . . .

.623 A publication which fails to comply with the requirements of this section within 10 days after notice by certified mail of the failure may not be mailed at the second-class rates of postage until it has come into compliance.

NOTES

CHAPTER ONE

1. Vernon W. Smith, "Studies in Control of Student Publications," in Herman A. Estrin and Arthur M. Sanderson (eds.), *Freedom and Censorship of the College Press* (Dubuque, Iowa: Wm. C. Brown, 1966), p. 189.

2. National Scholastic Press Association, *Helps*, Fall 1971, p. 3.

3. Frank Deaver, "Freedom and Responsibilities of the Junior College Newspaper," *Journalism Quarterly*, XLV (Autumn 1968), p. 550.

4. Buell G. Gallaher, "An Administrator Looks at the Campus Press," in Estrin and Sanderson, p. 98.

5. "College President Takes Anti-Censorship Stand," *Censorship Today*, Oct.-Nov. 1969, p. 27.

6. Robert J. Glessing, *The Underground Press in America* (Bloomington: Indiana University Press, 1970), p. 135.

7. Mark J. Green, "Too Young to Be Free," *The Progressive*, Jan. 1971, p. 28.

8. "Joint Statement on Rights and Freedoms of Students," *AAUP Bulletin*, Summer 1968, p. 260.

9. "Student Rights," *Education Digest*, Dec. 1968, p. 20.

10. "Excerpts from the Report of the Bar Association Commission," *Chronicle of Higher Education*, Feb. 24, 1970, p. 2.

11. "Toils of the College Press," *FOI Center Report* No. 180, May 1967, p. 6.

12. Don D. Horine, "How Principals, Advisers and Editors View the High School Newspaper," *Journalism Quarterly*, XLIII (Summer 1966), p. 339. Later studies indicate that censorship of secondary school publications is still widely practiced. Only 10 of 95 Arizona high school newspapers surveyed in 1969 had no censorship problems (Max H. James, "Propaganda or Education? Censorship and School Journalism," *Arizona English Bulletin*, XIII [Oct. 1970], p. 37). Three years later an opinion poll by the National Education Association showed that 70 percent of the nation's secondary school teachers believed in censorship of school-sponsored publications ("Censoring School Publications," *Today's Education*, LXI [Mar. 1972], p. 13).

13. Bruce M. Dudley, "Control of the Small College Student Newspaper," *Journalism Quarterly*, XLVI (Summer 1966), pp. 155–56.

14. 393 U.S. 503; 89 S. Ct. 733 (1969).

15. 307 F. Supp. 1328 (1969).

16. 286 F. Supp. 988 (1968); 415 F. 2d 860 (1969); 425 F. 2d 10 (1970); cert. denied, 400 U.S. 826, 91 S. Ct. 51 (1970).

17. 314 F. Supp. 832 (1970); 440 F. 2d 803 (1971). For more recent decisions similar to that of the U.S. Court of Appeals in *Eisner,* see Baughman v. Freinmuth, 343 F. Supp. 487 (1972); and Jacobs v. Board of School Commissioners of City of Indianapolis, 349 F. Supp. 605 (1972).

18. 453 F. 2d 54 (1971).

19. 462 F. 2d 1960 (1972).

20. 460 F. 2d 1355 (1972). The Seventh Circuit consists of Wisconsin, Illinois, and Indiana, and the *Fujishima* decision is binding in these states in the absence of a Supreme Court ruling on prior restraint in high schools. The *Eisner, Quarterman,* and *Shanley* decisions are binding in Connecticut, New York, and Vermont (Second Circuit); Maryland, West Virginia, Virginia, North Carolina, and South Carolina (Fourth Circuit); and Alabama, Florida, Georgia, Louisiana, Mississippi, and Texas (Fifth Circuit).

21. 273 F. Supp. 613 (1967).

22. 308 F. Supp. 1329 (1970).

23. 327 N.Y.S. 2d 755 (1971).

24. 322 F. Supp. 1266 (1971).

25. Eisner v. Stamford Board of Education, 314 F. Supp. 832 (1970). See also Sullivan v. Houston Independent School District, 307 F. Supp. 1328 (1969).

26. Glessing, p. 135. For a discussion of college rules on the distribution of printed material, see Morton M. Rosenfeld, "Campus Pamphleteering: The Emerging Constitutional Standard," 5 *University of Michigan Journal of Law Reform* 109 (1971).

27. New Left Education Project v. Board of Regents of the University of Texas System, A-69-CA-106 (Texas, 1970); "Regulation of Campus Paper Sales in Test," *Editor and Publisher,* Mar. 20, 1971, p. 29.

28. The Supreme Court held that the convening of the three-judge panel was improper, so the judgment was vacated and the case remanded. A three-judge court is required when the challenged regulation has statewide application, the Court pointed out, and this Texas regulation applied to only three of the state's universities. Board of Regents of the University of Texas System v. New Left Education Project, 40 U.S.L.W. 4167 (1972).

29. 317 F. Supp. 688 (1970).

30. 298 F. Supp. 238 (1969). See also Graham v. Houston Independent School District, 335 F. Supp. 1164 (1970). Graham indicates that if school rules are reasonably fair and student due process rights are upheld, the fact that high school students "flaunt" school rules is reason enough to reprimand them for distributing unauthorized printed material. In this case a school principal told students to leave school until their "attitudes changed." The court found this action reasonable.

31. 438 F. 2d 1058 (1971).

32. 480 P. 2d 766 (1971).

33. Robert Trager, "Freedom of the Press in College and High School," 35 *Albany Law Review* 161, 171 (1971).

34. 419 F. 2d 195 (1969); cert. denied, 399 U.S. 906, 90 S. Ct. 2191 (1970).

35. "High Court Told Colleges Need Clear and Present Danger Rule," *Civil Liberties,* Mar. 1970, p. 2. However, the Supreme Court declined to review the Norton decision (see note 34).

36. See Richard Cardwell, "The Law and the Student Press," *The Collegiate Journalist,* Fall 1968, p. 6; Robert C. Schubert, "State Action and the Private University," 24 *Rutgers Law Review* 323 (1970).

37. *Helps,* Fall 1971, p. 1.

38. 476 P. 2d 481 (1970). *Jergeson* might be compared with In the Matter of John Sklarsky, New York City Public School Chancellor's Decision, July 20, 1971. The chancellor upheld the censorship of libelous, obscene, or inflammatory items in school-sponsored publications but ruled that advisers and principals should not

censor an item because they disagree with its accuracy or tone. For the text of this decision see *School Press Review*, Oct. 1971, pp. 3–4, 12.

39. Trager, p. 180.

40. Schwartz v. Schuker, 298 F. Supp. 238 (1969).

41. "High Schools Are Rushing into Print—and Court," *Nation's Schools*, Jan. 1969, p. 30.

42. See Mary Moudry, "The Worst Censorship Is Hidden," *College Press Review*, Fall 1969, pp. 9–10.

43. Kenneth S. Devol, "Major Areas of Conflict in the Control of College and University Student Daily Newspapers in the United States," unpublished Ph.D. dissertation, Univ. S. Calif., 1965, pp. 162–63.

44. Linda Gregory, "Controls Exercised by Advisers of Indiana High School Newspapers," *Journalism Abstracts*, 1971, p. 117.

45. Annette Gibbs, "Ten Guidelines for Deans and a Free Student Press," *Syllabus*, Winter 1971, p. 7.

46. Robert Trager and Ron Ostman, "Tools for Caging the Censorship Dragon," *Scholastic Editor*, Feb. 1971, pp. 28–31. See also Trager and Ostman, "Caging the Censorship Dragon," *Scholastic Editor*, Dec. 1970-Jan. 1971, pp. 8–11.

47. National Association of Secondary School Principals, *Legal Memorandum*, Oct. 1971, p. 5.

48. "Bar Association Report Excerpts," p. 2.

49. National Council of College Publication Advisers, *Newsletter*, Nov. 1971, p. 4.

50. *Helps*, Fall 1971, pp. 3–4.

51. "Scratching from the Editor's Pen," *Quill and Scroll*, Oct.-Nov. 1971, p. 2.

CHAPTER TWO

1. John C. Merrill, "The Student Editor Needs a Clear-cut Policy from the Administration," in Herman A. Estrin and Arthur M. Sanderson (eds.), *Freedom and Censorship of the College Press* (Dubuque, Iowa: Wm. C. Brown, 1966), p. 110.

2. "Advise and Dispense," *Syllabus*, Spring 1971, p. 20.

3. Vernon W. Smith, "Studies in Control of Student Publications," in Estrin and Sanderson, p. 168.

4. John Behrens, "Legal Review," *College Press Review*, Spring 1971, p. 13.

5. William L. Prosser, *Handbook of the Law of Torts*, 4th ed. (St. Paul: West Publishing Co., 1971), pp. 984–85; Lee O. Garber and E. Edmund Reutter, *Yearbook of School Law, 1970* (Danville, Ill.: Interstate Printers and Publishers, 1970), p. 92.

6. See E. C. Bolmeier (ed.), *Legal Issues in Education* (Charlottesville, Va.: Michie Co., 1970), pp. 203–5.

7. Thomas Blackwell, *College Law* (Washington: American Council on Education, 1961), p. 189. A similar problem is presented by student body associations and other quasi-legal school organizations. Such organizations may or may not be suable entities, depending in part on a court's interpretation of the control exercised over them by an educational institution. See Lee O. Garber and E. Edmund Reutter, *Yearbook of School Law, 1969* (Danville, Ill.: Interstate Printers and Publishers, 1969), pp. 127–29.

8. 318 S.W. 2d 568 (1959); Smith, p. 166.

9. R. W. Tudor,, "Libel and the School Press," *College Press Review*, Spring 1965, p. 4.

10. Prosser, p. 775.

11. Kern Alexander, "Tort Liability Spreads to Students, Faculty," *Nation's Schools*, Mar. 1971, p. 55.

12. M. Chester Nolte and John Phillip Linn, *School Law for Teachers* (Danville, Ill.: Interstate Printers and Publishers, 1963), p. 246.

13. Prosser, p. 997.

14. Ibid.

15. Lawrence G. Weiss, "Goldwater and Colorado U.," *The Nation*, Dec. 8, 1962, pp. 402–4; "Toils of the College Press," *FOI Center Report* No. 180, May 1967, p. 2; Smith, pp. 174–75.

16. John S. Corcoran, "Libel and Private College Newspapers," *School and Society*, Oct. 1970, pp. 354–55.

17. "Prof Termed 'Phoney' Asks Libel Balm," *Editor and Publisher*, Jan. 2, 1965, p. 12; Robert E. Blackmon, "Case Against the *College Times*," *College Press Review*, Winter 1966, pp. 3–5, 12.

18. Langford v. Vanderbilt University, 287 S.W. 2d 32 (1956); 318 S.W. 2d 568 (1959); Robert H. Phelps and E. Douglas Hamilton, *Libel* (New York: Collier Books, 1966), pp. 221–23.

19. Case 63, Student Press in America Archives (Utica College, N.Y.).

20. 418 P. 2d 404 (1966); Charles Tribolett, "Case Against the *Arizona Wildcat*," *College Press Review*, Winter 1966, pp. 3, 12–14; Richard Cardwell, "Law and the Student Press," *The Collegiate Journalist*, Fall 1968, pp. 6–7.

21. Robert Trager, "Freedom of the Press in College and High School," 35 *Albany Law Review* 181 (1971). See also Schwartz v. Schuker, 298 F. Supp. 238 (1969), in which a U.S. District Court ruled: "Gross disrespect and contempt for the officials of an educational institution may be justification not only for suspension but also expulsion of a student [from a high school]." And in Segall v. Jacobson, 295 F. Supp. 1121 (1969), a U.S. District Court upheld the right of high school officials to transfer a student to another school because he distributed a forged issue of the school newspaper containing "libelous and scurrilous material."

22. Clifton O. Lawhorne, *Defamation of Public Officials* (Carbondale, Ill.: Southern Illinois University Press, 1971), p. 278.

23. Dale R. Spencer, "Are You Liable to Libel?" *Communication: Journalism Education Today*, Fall 1970, p. 15.

24. Dennis O. Gray, "Press Law Professor Acquires On-Job Experience—He's Sued," *Journalism Educator*, XXVI (Summer 1971), pp. 13–18.

25. *Purdue Exponent*, Oct. 30, 1968; "Defamation Suits Filed by University Policemen," *FOI Digest*, Nov.-Dec. 1968, p. 2; Letter from Richard Cardwell, Nov. 16, 1971.

26. 282 A. 2d 445 (1971).

27. "College Editor Charged with Criminal Libel," *Editor and Publisher*, Oct. 4, 1969, p. 20; Case 26, Student Press in America Archives (Utica College, N.Y.).

28. Tudor, pp. 4–5.

29. *New York Times*, Sept. 26, 1962; Samuel Feldman, *The Student Journalist and Legal and Ethical Issues* (New York: Richards Rosen Press, 1968), pp. 21–22.

30. Mele v. Cuddy, Essex County Court, Newark, N.J. (1970).

31. Newark *News*, Mar. 18, 1970; Newark *Star-Ledger*, Mar. 18, 1970.

32. Kern Alexander et al., *Public School Law* (St. Paul: West Publishing Co., 1969), p. 379. Public school employees might also have some protection in a libel suit if their states have public employee tort immunity statutes. But such statutes may primarily protect teachers in matters relating to school discipline or the supervision of students on school grounds or on field trips. See, for example, Mancha v. Field Museum of Natural History, 283 N.E. 2d 899 (1972), and Illinois Revised Statutes 85, 2-202 and 122, 24-24 (1965).

33. *New York Times*, June 2, 1970.

34. Garber and Reutter, *Yearbook of School Law, 1970*, pp. 99–100.

35. Gray, p. 18.

36. "Advise and Dispense," *Syllabus*, Fall 1971, p. 13.

37. Alexander, "Tort Liability," p. 55.

38. Cardwell, p. 7.

39. William Alfred, "The Law and the School Editor," in Gene Gilmore (ed.), *High School Journalism Today* (Danville, Ill.: Interstate Printers and Publishers, 1967), p. 107.

40. Kenneth S. Devol, "Libel and the Student Press," *The Collegiate Journalist,* Winter 1966, p. 12.

CHAPTER THREE

1. Robert C. McClure and William B. Lockhart, "Censorship of Obscenity: The Developing Constitutional Standard," 45 *Minnesota Law Review* 68 (1960).

2. Robert J. Glessing, *The Underground Press in America* (Bloomington: Indiana University Press, 1970), p. 148.

3. "Ginzburg: Intent of the Purveyor," *FOI Center Report* No. 182, June 1967, p. 3.

4. "Student Newspapers Should Be Free, Accurate, and Fair," *School and Society,* Oct. 1970, p. 327.

5. People v. Wasserman, 27 Mich. App. 16; 183 N.W. 2d 313 (1970).

6. L. Paul Kluzak, "Wasserman Test Fails; Obscenity Ruling Upheld," *Syllabus,* Fall 1971, p. 6.

7. Baker v. Downey City Board of Education, 307 F. Supp. 517 (1969). A similar case, Schwartz v. Schuker, 298 F. Supp. 238 (1969), produced a comparable result. The court said that a student's actions in distributing an underground newspaper on campus in violation of school regulations comprised "a pattern of open and flagrant defiance of school discipline."

8. Samuel Feldman, "Going Underground," *Communication: Journalism Education Today,* Fall 1970, pp. 11–12.

9. Vought v. Van Buren Public Schools, 306 F. Supp. 1388 (1969). See also Koppell v. Levine, 347 F. Supp. 456 (1972), in which a U.S. District Court held that because a high school literary magazine was not legally obscene, it could not be impounded by school officials.

10. Papish v. Board of Curators of the University of Missouri, 331 F. Supp. 1321 (1971); 464 F. 2d 136 (1972); 41 U.S.L.W. 3496 (1973).

11. "ACLU Asks USSC to Review Dismissal of U. of Mo. Student," *FOI Digest,* July-Aug. 1972, p. 2.

12. *New York Times,* Apr. 29, 1972; Koppell v. Levine, 347 F. Supp. 456 (1972).

13. "Frank Gill Quits Teaching Job, 'Disgusted' with College Paper," *Editor and Publisher,* Mar. 1, 1969, p. 12.

14. Fred Star, "Uproar Hits the Campus Press," *Look,* Feb. 18, 1969, p. 40.

15. "Frank Gill," p. 12.

16. "Student Press Revisited," *FOI Center Report* No. 260, Apr. 1971, p. 3.

17. Dario Politella, "The Campus Press and Confrontation Politics," *College Press Review,* Fall 1969, p. 7.

18. "Wave of Smut Charges," *Censorship Today,* April-May 1969, p. 25.

19. Korn v. Elkins, 317 F. Supp. 138 (1970).

20. In Ginzburg v. U.S., 383 U.S. 463 (1966), the Court affirmed the conviction of commercial publisher Ralph Ginzburg, holding in part that when it is unclear whether the work is obscene, evidence that the defendant intended to "pander to prurient interest" would help to sustain the conviction. The decision involved the aspect of commercialization in the advertising and sale of materials alleged to be obscene. Ginzburg had tried to get mailing privileges for a magazine *Eros* and other publications at Intercourse and Blue Ball, Pa., but facilities at these offices were too small and mailing privileges were denied. Ginzburg then settled on Middlesex, N.J.

21. Miller v. California, 41 U.S.L.W. 4925 (1973). The Supreme Court modified the previous test by making it clear that local community standards rather than

national apply in determining whether or not the material, taken as a whole, appeals to a prurient interest. Also, the Court indicated that juries and judges no longer need find that material is "utterly" without redeeming social value before declaring it obscene. Instead, juries and judges should make decisions on the basis of whether or not the work "taken as a whole lacks serious literary, artistic, political, or scientific value."

22. "Underground Wins Fed. Obscenity Case," *Civil Liberties,* Dec. 1970, p. 2.

23. 39 U.S.C., Sec. 4009. An advertisement is considered pandering if it offers to sell material which is, in the opinion of the recipient, "erotically arousing or sexually provocative." The material can be in the form of a display, classified, or editorial-style advertisement.

24. 308 F. Supp. 1329 (1970).

CHAPTER FOUR

1. State v. Buchanan, 250 Or. 244 (1968), cert. denied, 392 U.S. 905, 88 S. Ct. 2055 (1968).

2. California Evidence Code, 1070 (1966). At this writing this statute was in the process of being revised to protect newsmen called to testify at grand jury proceedings. The U.S. Supreme Court's 1972 decision in Branzburg v. Hayes, U.S. v. Caldwell, and In the Matter of Paul Pappas (33 L. Ed. 2d 626) involving professional reporters did not abrogate state shield laws. The high court simply held that newsmen have no inherent constitutional right to protect news sources in grand jury proceedings. The Court noted that Congress and state legislatures are still free to "determine whether a statutory newsman's privilege is necessary or desirable." No newsman has shield protection in congressional proceedings or in federal courts.

3. Louisiana Statutes, 45:1451 (1971); New Mexico Statutes, 20-1-12.1 (1970); General Laws of Rhode Island, 9-19.1-1 (1971).

4. Illinois Annotated Statutes, 77-1623 (1971).

5. Indiana Statutes, 2-1733 (1968). At this writing a more liberal shield law had been passed by the legislature and was awaiting the governor's signature.

6. Pennsylvania Statutes Annotated, 45.3 (1964).

7. New York Civil Rights Law, 79-h (1970).

8. Alaska Statutes, 09.25.220 (1970); Illinois Annotated Statutes, 77-1623 (1971); New Mexico Statutes, 20-1-12.1 (1970). Illinois and New Mexico also protect a person who edits news for publication.

9. Indiana Statutes, 2-1733 (1968).

10. New York Civil Rights Law, 79-h (1970).

11. Alaska Statutes, 09.25.168 (1970); Arkansas Statutes, 43-917 (1947); Illinois Annotated Statutes, 77-1623 (1971); Louisiana Statutes, 45:1451 (1971); New Mexico Statutes, 20-1-12.1 (1970).

12. 299 F. Supp. 102 (1969).

13. 306 F. Supp. 1097 (1969).

14. 183 N.W. 2d 93 (1971).

15. The *Caldwell* decision was appealed to the U.S. Supreme Court (see note 2 above), and the high court reversed the court of appeals, striking down the "compelling or overriding need" rule with regard to grand jury appearances. Newsmen have the same obligations as other citizens to testify before grand juries if so ordered, said the Court. However, in this decision the Supreme Court did not rule on the constitutional status of inanimate materials.

16. "Toils of the College Press," *FOI Center Report* No. 180, May 1967, p. 2.

17. L. Paul Kluzak, "Wasserman Test Fails; Obscenity Ruling Upheld," *Syllabus,* Fall 1971, p. 6.

18. "The Record," *The Quill,* July 1971, p. 13.

19. "Stanford *Daily* Editors Sue After Raid," *Publisher's Weekly,* June 14, 1971, p. 33.

20. "Police Search of Campus Paper Declared Illegal," *Editor and Publisher,* Oct. 14, 1972, p. 11.

21. Associated Press report, Nov. 10, 1972.

CHAPTER FIVE

1. Kenneth S. Devol, "Major Areas of Conflict in the Control of College and University Student Daily Newspapers in the United States," unpublished Ph.D. dissertation, Univ. S. Calif., 1965, p. 200.

2. 299 F. Supp. 102 (1969).

3. 306 F. Supp. 1097 (1969); 441 F. 2d 1257 (1971).

4. National Council of College Publication Advisers, *Newsletter,* Sept. 1967, p. 5.

5. Dario Politella, "Classic Cases of Campus Censorship," *College Press Review,* Spring 1971, p. 11.

6. See "Abortion Ads Aborted," *Syllabus,* Fall 1971, pp. 9, 12–13. Most of the advertisements were furnished by National Education Advertising Services, representative of some 900 college newspapers. By Dec. 1, 1970, NEAS had sent abortion referral ads to 780 of its clients. Only about 150 of them had refused to run such ads (Ibid., p. 9).

7. Florida Statutes Annotated, 797.02 (1965).

8. "Student Charged for Abortion List," *The Quill,* Nov. 1971, p. 33; Reg Crowder, "Charges Dropped Against Florida College Editor," *The Quill,* Jan. 1972, p. 27. The Florida Supreme Court affirmed the county court decision. State v. Sachs, 260 So. 2d 517 (1972).

9. 385 F. 2d 151 (1967).

CHAPTER SIX

1. 17 U.S.C. sect. 5 (1964).

2. Merwin G. Fairbanks, "Copyrighting the College Yearbook," *College Press Review,* Spring 1971, p. 8.

3. Fred S. Siebert, *Copyrights, Clearances, and Rights of Teachers in the New Educational Media* (Washington: American Council on Educaton, 1964).

4. Ibid. Many experts maintain that 50 words of material in copyright may be quoted without acquiring permission. Others say as many as 400 words may be used safely. However, if infringement is charged, each case is decided on its own merits. For example, copying one line of a short poem may not be "fair use."

5. R. R. Hamilton, "The Use of Copyrighted Material by Schools," *National School Law Reporter,* XII (Sept. 1962), p. 1. See also Marian Halley, "The Educator and the Copyright Law," in *Copyright Law Symposium Number Seventeen* (New York: Columbia University Press, 1969), pp. 24–50.

6. Wihtol v. Crow, 199 F. Supp. 682 (1961); 309 F. 2d 777 (1962). After finding for the plaintiff, the court of appeals returned the case to the district court for further proceedings. Damages in a copyright suit normally range from $250 to $5,000, plus any profits made from the infringement. In addition, the infringer may have to pay court costs and the plaintiff's attorney's fees.

7. Margaret Nicholson, *A Manual of Copyright Practice,* 2nd ed. (New York: Oxford University Press, 1970), p. 119. For more specific information on copyright see Nicholson; or write Head of Information and Publications Section, Copyright Office, Library of Congress, Washington, D.C. 20540.

8. For example, Executive Memorandum A-302, Purdue Univ., Apr. 1, 1971. The university retains patents and copyrights on inventions and publications when there is "substantial use of university funds or facilities."

CHAPTER SEVEN

1. As of 1971, all states except Delaware, Maryland, Mississippi, New Hampshire, New York, Rhode Island, South Carolina, Texas, and West Virginia had open records laws. States without open meetings laws were Kansas, Kentucky, Mississippi, Missouri, New York, North Carolina, Oregon, Rhode Island, South Carolina, Tennessee, West Virginia, and Wyoming. See "Sixteen States Fail to Adopt FOI Laws," *FOI Digest*, Jan.-Feb. 1971, p. 6.

2. Frank W. Rucker and Herbert Lee Williams, *Newspaper Organization and Management* (Ames: Iowa State University Press, 1955), p. 381.

3. Harold C. Nelson and Dwight L. Teeter, *Law of Mass Communications* (Mineola, N.Y.: Foundation Press, 1969), p. 390.

4. Harold L. Cross, *The People's Right to Know* (New York: Columbia University Press, 1953), p. 65.

5. See Bend Pub. Co. v. Hanner, 118 Or. 105, 244 P. 868 (1926); Hardman v. Collector of Taxes of North Adams, 317 Mass. 439, 58 N.E. 2d 845 (1945).

6. See State ex. rel. Halloran v. McGrath, 104 Mont. 490, 67 P. 2d 838 (1937).

7. "College Newspapers Face Challenges by School Administrations, Black Students," *FOI Digest*, Jan.-Feb. 1971, p. 6. The incident occurred at Pennsylvania State University. Details of the closed BSU meeting were obtained by the reporter by eavesdropping, and the BSU complained its right of privacy had been abridged. The Sigma Delta Chi chapter, on the other hand, said the "right to know" superseded the "right of privacy."

8. Wilbur Schramm, *Responsibility in Mass Communication* (New York: Harper & Brothers, 1957), p. 194.

9. Ibid., p. 196.

10. Sanchez v. Board of Regents of Eastern New Mexico University, 82 N.M. 672; 486 P. 2d 608 (1971).

11. "Court Seals University's Salary List," *Editor and Publisher*, June 19, 1971, p. 22.

12. "Degree of Openness Varies Widely at Trustee Meetings," *FOI Digest*, July-Aug. 1970, p. 2.

13. Ibid.

14. Cross, p. 119.

15. "Court Rules Equal Treatment for Underground and Established Press," *FOI Digest*, Nov.-Dec. 1971, p. 8. A U.S. District Court in Iowa ruled that the equal protection and due process clauses of the Fourteenth Amendment make the discrimination between reporters illegal. Quad-City Community News Service, Inc. v. Jebens, 40 U.S.L.W. 2315 (1971).

16. "Police Passes for Student Journalists?" *The Quill*, Apr. 1971, p. 3.

17. Ibid. The seven who do not issue passes: Philadelphia, Baltimore, New York, Houston, Chicago, St. Louis, and Cincinnati. The five who do: Dallas, Detroit, Kansas City, New Orleans, and Pittsburgh. The noncommittal: Cleveland, Denver, and Boston.

18. Bill McCloskey, "McCloskey Report," *Journal of College Radio*, Dec. 1971-Jan. 1972, p. 18.

CHAPTER EIGHT

1. For example, the New York City public school chancellor noted In the Matter of John Sklarsky that "the principal is ultimately responsible for the content of official school publications." See *School Press Review*, Oct. 1971, p. 4.

2. Donald R. Grubb, "A Modified Integrated Approach," in Herman A. Estrin and Arthur M. Sanderson (eds.), *Freedom and Censorship of the College Press* (Dubuque, Iowa: Wm. C. Brown, 1966), p. 44.

3. Robert Tager and Ron Ostman, "Caging the Censorship Dragon," *Scholastic Editor,* Dec. 1970-Jan. 1971, pp. 8–11.

4. Orley R. Herron and Edward E. Ericson, "How to Organize Control of Your Student Publications," *College and University Business,* Oct. 1967, pp. 8–10.

5. "A Brief for Abolishing Publishing Boards," *Syllabus,* Fall 1970, p. 12.

6. Robert J. Glessing, *The Underground Press in America* (Bloomington: Indiana University Press, 1970), p. 53.

7. "The Student Newspaper: Activity or Laboratory?" *College Press Review,* Spring 1971, pp. 13–19.

8. John B. Wood, "College Newspapers—Northeast," in American Council on Education, *The Student Newspaper* (Washington, D.C., 1970), p. 33.

9. Roger Ebert, "Plain Talk on College Newspaper Freedom," in Estrin and Sanderson, p. 117; John Behrens, "Legal Review," *College Press Review,* Winter 1970–71, p. 19; Noel Greenwood, "The Daily Cal Leaves Campus. Who's Next?" *The Quill,* Dec. 1971, pp. 14–15; "Changes Are Proposed for Student Newspaper," *Editor and Publisher,* Mar. 8, 1969, p. 24; "Advise and Dispense," *Syllabus,* Fall 1971, p. 2; "Ithaca's Student Newspaper Becomes a Corporation," *College Press Review,* Fall 1969, p. 27.

10. *AAUP Bulletin,* Summer 1968, p. 260.

11. "Guidelines for the Student Press: The View from Chapel Hill," *Syllabus,* Summer 1971, pp. 6–8.

12. An Idaho Supreme Court decision upheld a lower court ruling which had declared activity fees charged students as unconstitutional. A high school student had refused to pay $25 activity fee for textbooks and activities, contending that the fee requirement denied him of the "free common schools" guaranteed in the Idaho Constitution. The high court said that fees could be charged for only those extracurricular activities in which students chose to participate. Paulson v. Minidoka County School District No. 331, 463 P. 2d 935 (1970).

13. "Guidelines . . ." *Syllabus,* Summer 1971, pp. 6–8.

14. Purdue Exponent Review Board Report, Jan. 19, 1969, p. 12.

15. Ibid., p. 59.

16. "Student Charged for Abortion List," *The Quill,* Nov. 1971, p. 33; Reg Crowder, "Charges Dropped Against Florida College Editor," *The Quill,* Jan. 1972, p. 27; State v. Sachs, 260 So. 2d 517 (1972).

17. Ted Dellinger, "Alligator Wrestling for a Free Press at U. of Florida," *Purdue Exponent,* Oct. 3, 1972; "Students Maintain Control over U. of Florida Paper," *FOI Digest,* Sept.-Oct. 1972, p. 7; Mark Mehler, "Florida U. Prexy Orders Student Paper off Campus," *Editor and Publisher,* Jan. 13, 1973, p. 10.

18. Thomas Blackwell, *College Law* (Washington: American Council on Education, 1961), p. 189.

19. Louis J. Berman, "Rx: Incorporation, No Panacea," *Scholastic Editor,* Dec. 1971-Jan. 1972, p. 15.

20. Ibid.

21. Bill G. Ward, *The Student Press 1971* (New York: Richards Rosen Press, 1971), pp. 123–24.

CHAPTER NINE

1. "Toils of the College Press," *FOI Center Report* No. 180, May 1967, p. 1.

2. See "Seizure of Allegedly Obscene Material—Requirement of a Prior Adversary Hearing," 32 *Ohio State Law Journal* 668 (1971). In some situations, courts have allowed the seizure of such material without a prior hearing if time is an important consideration and the material might be destroyed.

3. "The Underground Press," *FOI Center Report* No. 226, Aug. 1969, p. 5.

4. Strasser v. Doorley, 309 F. Supp. 716 (1970); 432 F. 2d 567 (1970).

5. Lafayette (Ind.) *Journal and Courier,* Sept. 21, 1971.
6. Ibid., Oct. 20, 1971.
7. Ibid., Sept. 12, 1972.
8. 307 F. Supp. 517 (1969).
9. 462 F. 2d 960 (1972).

CHAPTER TEN

1. *New York Times,* Dec. 21, 1970.
2. U.S. Dept. of the Treasury, Internal Revenue Service, *Code,* Sect. 501 (c) (3). Exemption from Taxation: "Corporations . . . organized and operated exclusively for . . . educational purposes . . . no part of the net earnings of which inures to the benefit of any private shareholder, . . . and which does (do) not participate in . . . any political campaign on behalf of any candidate for public office."
3. *Higher Education and National Affairs,* American Council on Education, June 11, 1971, p. 7.
4. Ibid.
5. Ibid.
6. "Student Press Revisited," *FOI Center Report* No. 260, Apr. 1971, p. 4.
7. *New York Times,* Dec. 21, 1970.
8. *FOI Center Report* No. 260, p. 4.
9. Ibid.
10. Paula Simons, "How Much Editorial Freedom?" *Communication: Journalism Education Today,* Summer 1972, p. 15.
11. The Federal Communications Commission does not license carrier-current stations (those that broadcast through a modulated radio frequency signal, typically conducted along electrical lines to buildings on campus). Such stations have been exempt fom FCC regulations because they are capable of reaching only a specific audience within controllable bounds. Such stations must, however, comply with FCC-determined limits on radiation strength and make sure their signals radiate only a few feet from electrical wires. The FCC has considered the licensing of carrier-current stations. See "FCC Investigation and Regulation of College Carrier-Current Radio Stations," 8 *Columbia Journal of Law and Social Problems* 196 (1972).
12. Post v. Payton, 323 F. Supp. 799 (1971).
13. "College Radio News," *Journal of College Radio,* Mar. 1971, p. 16.
14. Robert J. Glessing, *The Underground Press in America* (Bloomington: Indiana University Press, 1970), p. 89.
15. U.S. Postal Service, *Postal Service Manual,* Ch. 1, Part 132.224. See also the discussion in Ch. 3 on the nonmailability of obscene material.
16. "Lottery News in the Press," *FOI Center Report* No. 233, Dec. 1969, p. 2.
17. U.S. Post Office Department, *The Law vs. Lotteries* (June 1963), p. 11.

NOTES ON SOURCES

THE *National Reporter System* for legal decisions was the basis for much of the research for this book. Other helpful sources are listed below.

BOOKS

Alexander, Kern, et al. *Public School Law*. St. Paul: West Publishing Co., 1969.

American Council on Education. *The Student Newspaper*. Washington, D.C.: The Council, 1970. A report by the Special Commission on the Student Press to the President of the University of California. Discusses the nature, role, and quality of student newspapers on University of California campuses. Examines such issues as how the student newspaper should be financed and supervised and what is "obscene" language.

Blackwell, Thomas. *College Law*. Washington, D.C.: American Council on Education, 1961.

Estrin, Herman A., and Arthur M. Sanderson (eds.). *Freedom and Censorship of the College Press*. Dubuque, Iowa: Wm. C. Brown, 1966. Emphasizes the philosophical and practical considerations of censorship but has some legal information. Vernon W. Smith's chapter on "Studies in Control of Student Publications" is especially good.

Feldman, Samuel. *The Student Journalist and Legal and Ethical Issues*. New York: Richards Rosen Press, 1968. A concentration on ethical problems, since most legal decisions involving the student press date from 1969.

Garber, Lee O., and E. Edmund Reutter, *Yearbook of School Law, 1970*. Danville, Ill.: Interstate Printers and Publishers, 1970. Updated yearly and has some valuable information on tort liability of teachers.

Glessing, Robert. *The Underground Press in America*. Bloomington: Indiana University Press, 1970.

Nolte, M. Chester, and John Phillip Linn. *School Law for Teachers.* Danville, Ill.: Interstate Printers and Publishers, 1963.

Prosser, William L. *Handbook of the Law of Torts,* 4th ed. St. Paul: West Publishing Co., 1971.

PERIODICALS

A number of periodicals run occasional articles on the law and the student press. Among the most useful: *Civil Liberties, College Press Review, Collegiate Journalist, Communication: Journalism Education Today, Editor and Publisher, Higher Education and National Affairs, Journal of College Radio, Journalism Educator, Nation's Schools, Publisher's Auxiliary, Quill, Quill and Scroll, Scholastic Editor, School and Society, School Press Review,* and *Syllabus.* Robert Trager's "Freedom of the Press in College and High School" in the 1971 *Albany Law Review* is a particularly good summary of censorship cases, 1967–1971.

References to specific periodical articles can be found in the Notes.

REPORTS AND DIGESTS

Freedom of Information Center (University of Missouri), *Reports* and *Digests.* The FOI keeps abreast of the student press and some of its legal problems.

National Association of Secondary School Principals' *Legal Memorandum.*

National Council of College Publications Advisers' *Newsletters.*

National Education Association Research Service, *Student's Day in Court* and *Teacher's Day in Court.* Annual reports that discuss major decisions during the previous year.

National Scholastic Press Association, *Helps.*

Student Press in America Archives, Utica College, Utica, N.Y. (John Behrens, curator.) A collation of cases, issues, and questions pertaining to the student press. Periodic reports on holdings are issued by Prof. Behrens.

BOOKS ON GENERAL PRESS LAW

The reader who needs more background in general press law will find the following helpful:

Ashley, Paul P. *Say It Safely; Legal Limits in Publishing, Radio, and Television,* 4th ed. Seattle: University of Washington Press, 1969. A widely used handbook.

Gillmor, Donald M., and Jerome A. Barron. *Mass Communication Law.* St. Paul: West Publishing Co., 1969, 1971 supplement.

Nelson, Harold L., and Dwight L. Teeter. *Law of Mass Communications.* Mineola, N.Y.: Foundation Press, 1969, 1971 notes.

INDEX OF CASES

Antonelli v. Hammond, 12–14, 55
Avins v. Rutgers University, 69
Baker v. Downey City Board of Education, 48–49, 98
Baughman v. Freinmuth, 144
Campus Alliance v. Iowa State *Daily*, 33–34
Channing Club v. Board of Regents of Texas Tech University, 16–17
Dickey v. Alabama State Board of Education, 11–12
Eisner v. Stamford Board of Education, 8–10, 144
Fujishima v. Board of Education, 10–11
Graham v. Houston Independent School District, 144
Jacobs v. Board of School Commissioners of City of Indianapolis, 144
Jergeson v. Board of Trustees of School District No. 7, 19–20
Katz v. McAuley, 17
Klahr v. Winterble, 35–36
Koppell v. Levine, 51–52, 147
Korn v. Elkins, 53–54
Langford v. Vanderbilt University, 32–33, 101
Lee v. Board of Regents, 60, 65–67
Mele v. Cuddy, 41
New Left Education Project v. Board of Regents of the University of Texas System, 15–16, 144
Norton v. Discipline Committee of East Tennessee State University, 18–19

Panarella v. Birenbaum, 14
Papish v. Board of Curators of University of Missouri, 50–51
Paulson v. Minidoka County School District No. 331, 151
People v. Wasserman, 47–48
Post v. Payton, 104–5
Quad City Community News Service, Inc., v. Jebens, 81, 150
Quarterman v. Byrd, 10
Sanchez v. Board of Trustees of Eastern New Mexico University, 79–80, 150
Scelfo v. Rutgers University, 39
Schwartz v. Schuker, 17, 145–47
Scoville v. Board of Education, 7–8
Segall v. Jacobson, 146
Shanley v. Northeast Independent School District, 10, 98–99
State v. Buchanan, 57–58
State v. Knops, 60–61
State v. Owen, 17–18
State v. Sachs, 68, 90
Strasser v. Doorley, 96–97, 151
Sullivan v. Houston Independent School District, 6–7, 144
Tinker v. Des Moines Independent School District, 5–6
Trujillo v. Love, 14–15
Vought v. Van Buren Public Schools, 50
Wihtol v. Crow, 74, 149
Zucker v. Panitz, 60, 64–65

155

INDEX OF NAMES

Adams, John B., 89
Adams, Ralph, 12
Alexander, Kern, 43
Alfred, William, 43
Althen, Gary, 30
American Association of University
    Professors, 4
American Bar Association, 4, 22
American Civil Liberties Union, 4, 18,
    21, 97
American Yearbook Company, 41
Antonelli, John, 13
Arizona, University of, 35
Arkansas, University of, 40
Association of American University Pro-
    fessors, 88
Auburn University, 12

Barringer, Felicity, 62
Becker, William H., Judge, 51
Behrens, John, 27
Benz, Lester G., 24
Berman, Louis J., 92
Bickerton, Irene, 40–41
Birenbaum, William, 4
Blackwell, Thomas, 28
Boston College, 88
Boston University, 93
Bronson, S. Jerome, Judge, 48
Brown, Richmond, 81
Buchanan, Annette, 57

Caldwell, Earl, 60
California, University of (Berkeley), 26,
    47, 53, 88
California State College, Los Angeles, 31
Cardwell, Richard, 38, 43
Chowka, Peter, 105
Ciervo, Arthur, 82
Cleaver, Eldridge, 13, 103

Colorado, University of, 29–30, 88
Columbia University, 93, 102–3
Cornell University, 61, 93
Crary, Avery, Judge, 48–49
Cuddy, Robert, 41
C. W. Post College, 104

Dartmouth College, 88
Devol, Kenneth, 43, 63
Dickey, Gary, 11–12
Doyle, James E., Judge, 66
Dumke, Glenn A., Chancellor, 103

Eastern New Mexico University, 80
East Tennessee State University, 18
Eisenhower, Dwight, 30
Ericson, Edward E., 86

Fitchburg (Mass.) State College, 13
Florida, University of, 68, 90
Florida State University, 67
Fortas, Abe, Justice, 6
Friedman, Philip, 31–32

Gallaher, Buell G., 4
Garity, W. Arthur, Judge, 13
Georgetown University, 81–82, 105
Gibbs, Annette, 22
Gill, Frank P., 52
Glessing, Robert, 4, 87
Goldwater, Barry, Senator, 30
Grand Valley State (Mich.) College, 47,
    61
Gray, Dennis O., 38, 42
Green, Mark J., 4
Gregory, Linda, 22
Gutierrez, Felix, 32

Hamilton, R. R., 73
Hammond, James J., 13
Harvard University, 88, 96
Herron, Orley R., 86

Illinois, University of, 88
Indiana University, 38, 43, 88
Iowa, University of, 88
Iowa State University, 33–34
Ithaca College, 90–91

Junior Red Cross, 17

Kansas, University of, 52
Klahr, Gary Peter, 35–36

Langford, Pamela, 33
Lawhorne, Clifton O., 37
Levine, Sol, 52
Linn, John Phillip, 29
Lockhart, William B., 46

McClure, Robert C., 46
Maryland, University of, 53
Maryland State Board of Education, 3, 23
Merced (Calif.) College, 53
Merrill, John C., 26
Metzer, Charles M., Judge, 65
Miller, Sherman, 36
Mills, Mary, 67
Minnesota, University of, 88
Missouri, University of, 50–51, 95
Mitcham, Carl, 30

National Association of Secondary School Principals, 22
National Scholastic Press Association, 19
Newton, Quigg, 30
New York Civil Liberties Union, 52
Nolte, M. Chester, 29
North Carolina, University of, 88–89
Northern Illinois University, 85

O'Connell, Stephen, 90
Ohio State University, 69
Ohio University, 40
Oregon, University of, 57
Ostman, Ron, 22, 86

Pacific University, 31
Panitz, Adolph, Dr., 64
Papish, Barbara Susan, 50–51

Peckham, Robert F., Judge, 62
Pennsylvania State University, 93
Prosser, William, 29
Purdue University, 88–90, 93, 97

Richmond College, 14
Rockefeller, Nelson, 103
Rose, Frank, 11–12
Rutgers University, 39, 69

Sachs, Ronald, 68
St. John's University, 103
San Jose State (Calif.) College, 103
Siebert, Fred S., 72
Sigma Delta Chi, 61, 78–79
Smith, Raymond L., Judge, 48
Smith, Vernon W., 3, 26
South Carolina, University of, 23
Southern Colorado State College, 14
Spencer, Dale R., 37
Stanford University, 61, 93
Staten Island Community College, 14
Students for a Democratic Society, 39

Texas, University of, 16
Texas Tech University, 16
Thornton, Thomas P., Judge, 50
Trager, Robert, 18, 20, 22, 36, 86
Trench, Benjamin M., Judge, 68
Trombley, Charles, 31
Troy State (Ala.) College, 11–12
Trujillo, Dorothy, 14–15
Tudor, R. W., 28

Utica College, 88

Vanderbilt University, 28, 33, 91, 101-2

Ward, Bill, 93
Wasserman, James, 47–48
Wayne State University, 52
Weinstein, Jack B., Judge, 52
Wichita State (Kans.) University, 87
Winterble, Peter, 36
Wisconsin State University, Whitewater, 60, 65–66

Yale University, 88
Yant, Marty, 81–82
Young Americans for Freedom, 39

Zampano, Robert C., Judge, 9
Zucker, Laura, 65